DEDICATION

This book is dedicated to Dr. John Hagee whose love of and proclamation of the truth has never wavered. America's survival owes much to this courageous man of God. He has faithfully wielded the sword of the Spirit for over 50 years. His life and legacy will stand the test of time and eternity.

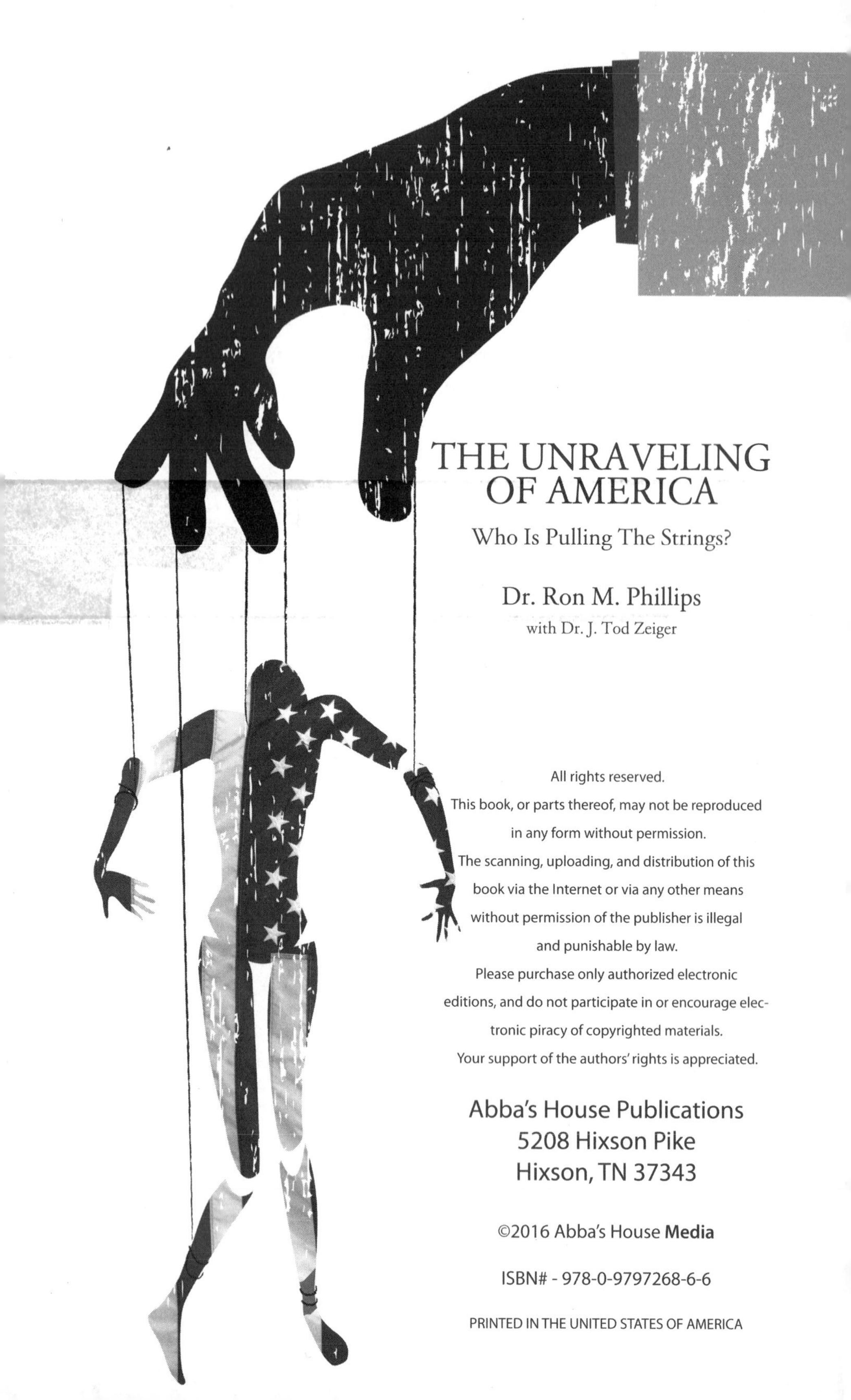

THE UNRAVELING OF AMERICA

Who Is Pulling The Strings?

Dr. Ron M. Phillips
with Dr. J. Tod Zeiger

Abba's House Publications
5208 Hixson Pike
Hixson, TN 37343

ISBN# - 978-0-9797268-6-6

PRINTED IN THE UNITED STATES OF AMERICA

ACKNOWLEDGEMENTS

I would like to thank my wife of 47 years, Reverend Paulette Phillips, for her encouragement to leave a legacy of truth for our grandchildren. To my son, Dr. Ronnie Phillips, Jr., and his willingness to take up this difficult mantle.

I wish to thank my dear friend, Dr. J. Tod Zeiger for all his hard work in researching and assisting me in getting the truth on paper.

Also, to the fine media staff at Abba's House whose passion for excellence inspires me. Special thanks to Angie McGregor and Dana Harding for their tireless editing, Julie Harding for proofing and Doug Wright for the layout and design of the book.

To Andrea Ridge who types my handwritten notes and undoubtedly has a gift to read my hasty script. God bless you all.

TABLE OF CONTENTS

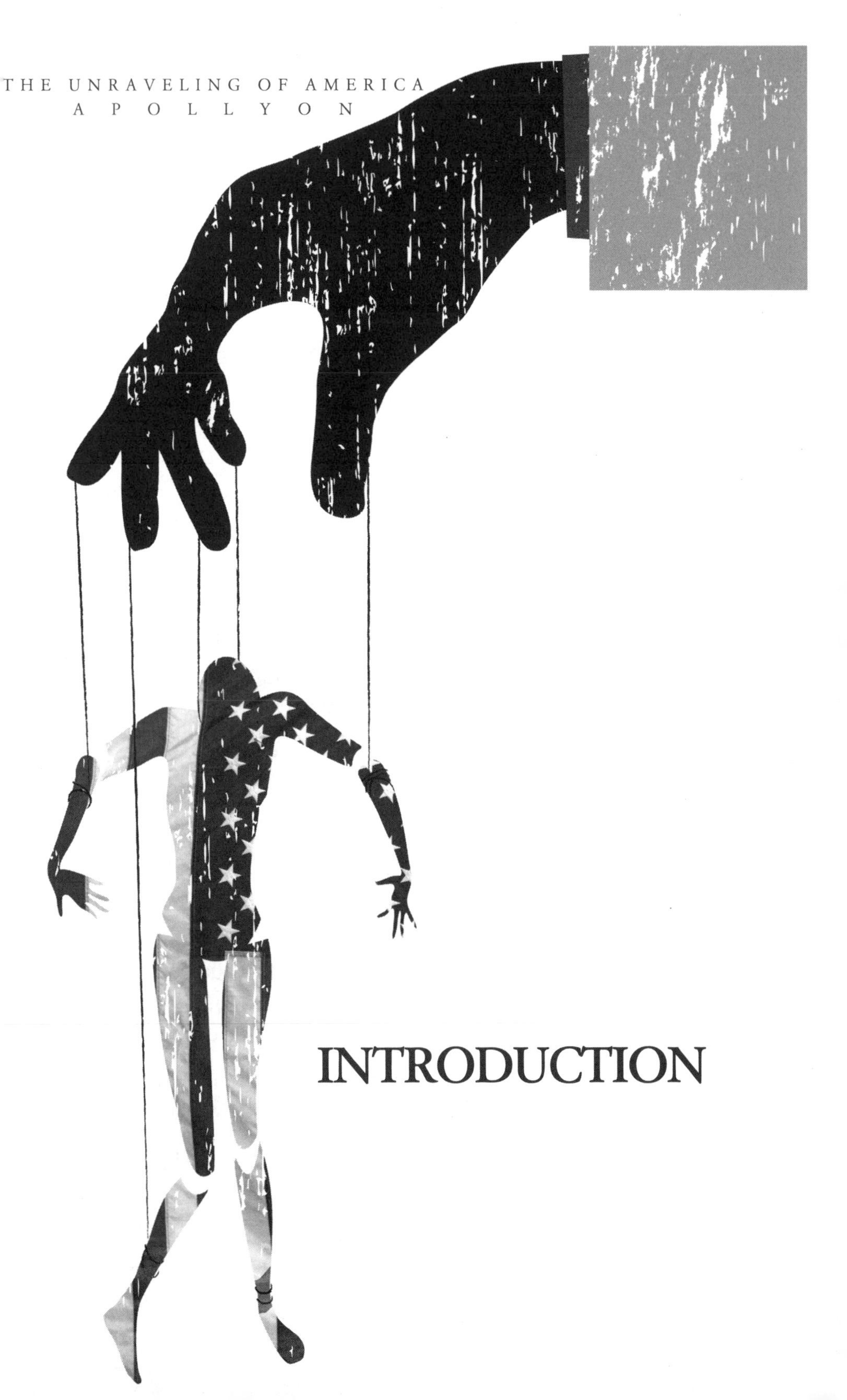

INTRODUCTION

After I was baptized in the Holy Spirit, the Lord sent me immediately to the spiritual battlefield. After two decades of warfare experiences and serious study of the Scriptures, I wrote *Everyone's Guide to Demons and Spiritual Warfare* which became a best seller. To my surprise, this life's work won the 2011 award as Charismatic Book of the Year.

Upon my incursion into spiritual warfare, a well-respected pastor of a large megachurch (and a dear friend), said, "You seem to be seeing a demon behind every bush." He laughed heartily. Shortly before his death he said to me, "Ron, you remember what I said to you about demons?" I responded, "Yes sir!" "Well," he said, "so far there has been a demon behind every bush I have encountered. Stay in the battle!" He smiled and went on.

St. Paul and the New Testament clearly declares that behind human government and societies are malevolent forces exercising an invisible war on humanity.

They are described in Ephesians, Colossians, and Romans as "principalities, powers, rulers of darkness, and spiritual forces of wickedness". These forces are arrayed over and within nations to oppose the coming of God's Kingdom.

It is my strong conviction that demonic interference and disruption threaten our western society. Like Islamic terror in the natural world, there exists invisible terror cells in the spiritual realm called strongholds.

From these fortresses of error come the lies and distortions that scripture says "destroys" God's people. The Bible identifies the leader of these dark forces as Apollyon – the destroyer.

And they had as king over them the angel of the bottomless pit, whose name in Hebrew is Abaddon, but in Greek he has the name Apollyon.
Revelation 9:11, NKJV

My people are destroyed for lack of knowledge.
Because you have rejected knowledge,
I also will reject you from being priest for Me;
Because you have forgotten the law of your God,
I also will forget your children.
Hosea 4:6, NKJV

This book illuminates the dark realm that has seized our politics, our culture and our media. Our task is not simply to expose "the lie", but to release the truth which alone can set humanity and our culture free!

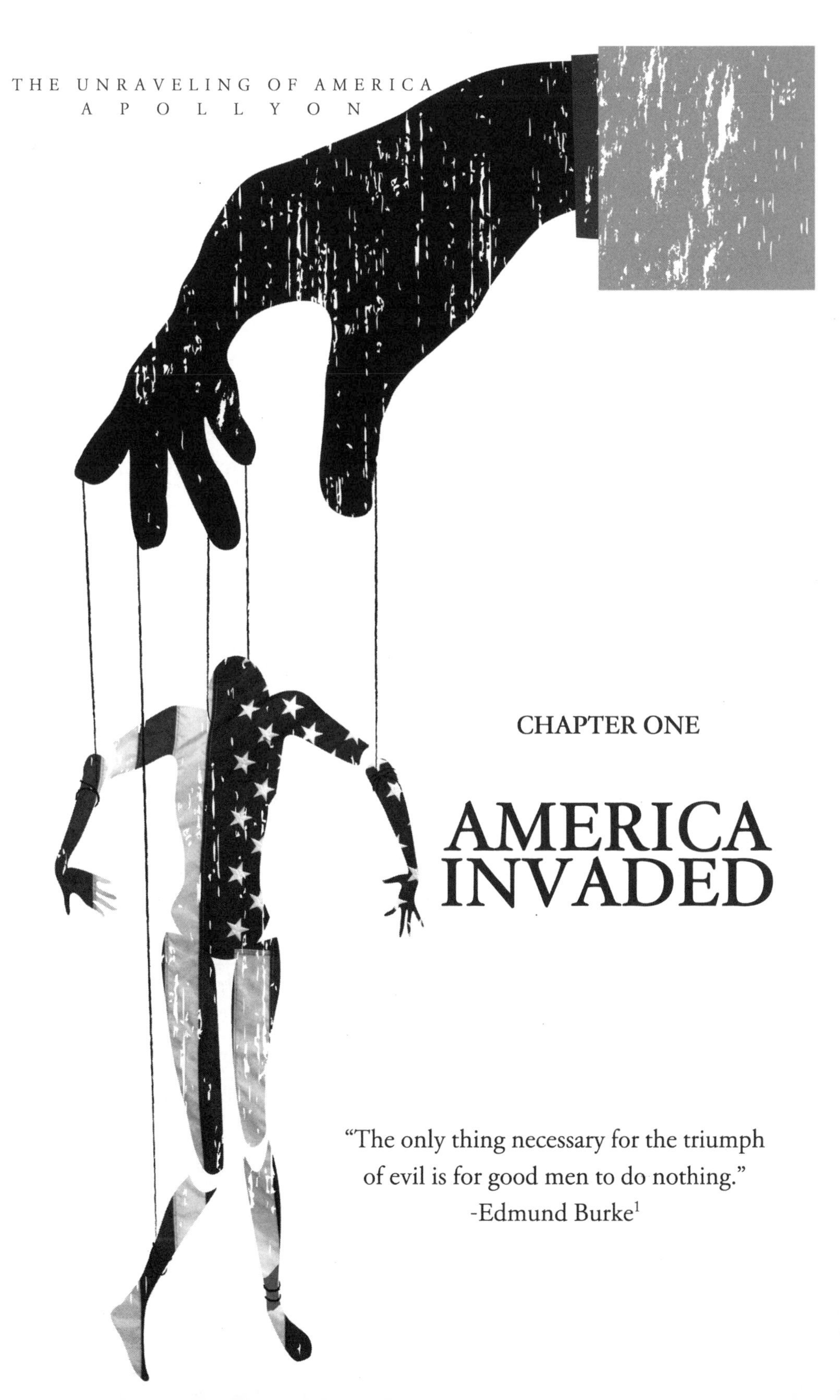

CHAPTER ONE

AMERICA INVADED

"The only thing necessary for the triumph of evil is for good men to do nothing."
-Edmund Burke[1]

As Americans, we have been blessed by the fact that, because we are bordered on the east by the Atlantic Ocean, on the west by the Pacific, and with the friendly nations of Canada and Mexico to our north and south, we have been relatively safe from hostile outside forces that would seek to invade and conquer our nation. With the exception of the American Revolutionary War and the War of 1812 (both having the British Empire as the aggressor), and the Japanese attack on Pearl Harbor during World War II, we have never been seriously threatened with all-out invasion by a national foreign power.

The term invasion usually denotes a strategic endeavor of substantial magnitude; because the goals of an invasion are usually large-scale and long-term. A sizable force is needed to hold territory and protect the interests of the invading entity.

Military operations that occur within the territory of a single geopolitical entity are sometimes termed "invasions" if armed forces enter into a well-defined part of that territory that, at the time of the operation, was completely under the control of armed forces of another faction as in a civil war or insurrection.

The term "invasion" does not denote the justification or morality of the aggressing military force, or whether they are motivated by good or evil intent. For example, two sets of World War II military operations—one by the Nazis against Poland in 1939, and the other by the Allies in Nazi-controlled France in 1944—are often called the Invasion of Poland and Invasion of Normandy, respectively. Both military operations are properly called invasions because they involved an outside force entering territory not under its authority or control at the time."[2]

Invasions that have occurred throughout history and around the world are so numerous it would be impossible to list them all in this book. However, one example that illustrates the fear and uncertainty of imminent invasion occurred in the United States immediately following the Japanese attack on Pearl Harbor on December 7, 1941. Although a Japanese invasion of the U.S. mainland did not happen, that in no way alleviated the fear and panic that it would happen at any minute!

The following account will give you some insight on just how real the fear had become:

"California was witness to some of the most traumatic events that happened during the war in the then 48 states. When Pearl Harbor was bombed on Dec. 7, 1941 California was racked from north to south with near panic conditions because tens of thousands of its citizens expected similar attacks, possibly by the same naval force that attacked Hawaii, at any time on California cities.

Within days of the attack on Hawaii, Japanese submarines were attacking merchant ships off California's coast reinforcing those fears. Wild rumors circulated of Japanese invasion fleets being seen in California water and of actual Japanese landings. There were rumors of air attacks, rumors that secret Japanese air bases existed in California's deserts or in Mexico, rumors of sabotage, of periscope sightings and of many other fearful things. Worst of all, there were wild and unfair rumors about the ethnic Japanese: Japanese fishermen were mining harbors, and supplying food, fuel and secret information to submarines off the coast; Japanese farmers were poisoning fruits and vegetables they brought to market; the Japanese were secretly organized into military units to carry out attacks behind American lines if and when an invasion came. None of these things were true, but every such rumor was believed by someone."[3]

ENEMIES INSIDE THE GATE

Joseph Goebbels was propaganda minister for Adolf Hitler in Nazi Germany. He was the man responsible for propagating the demonic lies that led to World War II and the slaughter of millions of innocent people, including six million Jews. He said, "If you tell a lie big enough and keep repeating it, people will eventually come to believe it. The lie can be maintained only for such time as the State can shield the people from the political, economic and/or military consequences of the lie. It thus becomes vitally important for the State to use all of its powers to repress dissent, for the truth is the mortal enemy of the lie, and thus by extension, the truth is the greatest enemy of the State."[4]

For at least the last decade America has repeatedly been fed "lies big enough" to now seem to be the truth to many citizens. Swallowing the propaganda of a progressive ideological agenda, our spiritual and moral base has eroded to the point that America is no longer recognized as the world's leader in moral and spiritual convictions. America has become a caricature of her former self!

It was Winston Churchill who said, "A lie gets halfway around the world before the truth has a chance to get its pants on."[5] It is time for us to "put on our pants" and tell the truth before it's too late. With twenty-four hour news cycles and a common stream of information on the internet, it is no longer acceptable to say, "I did not know what was going on."

No nation or civilization has ever survived the radical decline we are seeing at this present hour! Edward Gibbon's book, *Decline and Fall of the Roman Empire,* astonishingly parallels our own decline in America.

Listen to Gibbon as he speaks of the insidious termites that were eating away at the foundation of a decaying culture. He lists five marks of the decaying Roman culture:

1. Concern with displaying affluence instead of building wealth

2. Obsession with sex and perversions of sex
3. Art becomes freakish and sensationalistic instead of creative and original
4. Widening disparity between very rich and very poor
5. Increased demand to live off the state.

Gibbon goes on to say . . . "It was scarcely possible that the eyes of contemporaries should discover in the public felicity the latent causes of decay and corruption. This long peace, and the uniform government of the Romans, introduced a slow and secret poison into the vitals of the empire. The minds of men were gradually reduced to the same level, the fire of genius was extinguished, and even the military spirit evaporated. Their personal valour remained, but they no longer possessed that public courage which is nourished by the love of independence, the sense of national honour, the presence of danger, and the habit of command. They received laws and governors from the will of their sovereign, and trusted for their defense to a mercenary army. The posterity of their boldest leaders was contented with the rank of citizens and subjects. The most aspiring spirits resorted to the court or standard of the emperors; and the deserted provinces, deprived of political strength or union, insensibly sunk into the languid indifference of private life."[6]

Will America follow the footsteps of the Roman Empire? Will she permit the continual erosion of her proud heritage? I do not believe it will ever happen as long as we remember it is not just military might and economic strength that keep us safe and secure within our own borders.

America has lost its way morally and spiritually and that is where the danger lies. I contend that America has been invaded not by military forces, but by spiritual forces that are at work at this present hour to undermine the root system that has produced the fruit of freedom and liberty around the world. The bright light of the Gospel of Jesus Christ has shown in the darkest parts of the world simply because believers united in a common cause of sharing the good news of Jesus Christ.

The culture war is going on in every segment of society, from the board room to the class room, and from the White House to the church house. We are seeing a major shift in attitudes and actions that once defined us as the greatest nation on earth. Main-stream media has aided and abetted the ongoing nudging of America toward a progressive agenda, effectively lowering our moral and spiritual standards.

As the foundation grows weaker, the attacks on Christianity grow bolder and are seen in all parts of the world. War has been declared on Christianity in every part of the Middle East, with reports of Christians being beheaded at the bloody hand of ISIS (or ISIS related groups).

In America, the assault on the lives of Christians happens so often it has almost become commonplace to the masses. The assault on traditional values can best be seen in a recent survey conducted by Gallup. In May 2015, Gallup conducted a survey showing that Americans are becoming more liberal on social issues. Based on the responses of both conservative, liberal, and moderate Americans, the survey reports:

"Americans are becoming more liberal on social issues, as evidenced not only by the uptick in the percentage describing themselves as socially liberal, but also by their increasing willingness to say that a number of previously frowned-upon behaviors are morally acceptable. The biggest leftward shift over the past 14 years has been in attitudes toward gay and lesbian relations, from only a minority of Americans finding it morally acceptable to a clear majority finding it acceptable.

The moral acceptability of issues related to sexual relations has also increased, including having a baby outside of wedlock-- something that in previous eras was a social taboo. Americans are more likely to find divorce morally acceptable, and have also loosened up on their views of polygamy, although this latter behavior is still seen as acceptable by only a small minority.

This liberalization of attitudes toward moral issues is part of a complex set of factors affecting the social and cultural fabric of the U.S. Regardless of the factors causing the shifts, the trend toward a more liberal view on moral behaviors will certainly have implications for such fundamental social institutions as marriage, the environment in which children are raised, and the economy. The shifts could also have a significant effect on politics, with candidates whose positioning is based on holding firm views on certain issues having to grapple with a voting population that, as a whole, is significantly less likely to agree with conservative positions than it might have been in the past."[7]

PULL BACK THE CURTAIN

While on the Isle of Patmos, the apostle John was given a prophetic picture of the last days–the end of the age. In Revelation 9, he introduces us to a frightening character, Apollyon: The Destroyer.

> *Then the fifth angel sounded: And I saw a star fallen from heaven to the earth. To him was given the key to the bottomless pit. And he opened the bottomless pit, and smoke arose out of the pit like the smoke of a great furnace. So the sun and the air were darkened because of the smoke of the pit. Then out of the smoke locusts came upon the earth. And to them was given power, as the scorpions of the earth have power. They were commanded not to harm the grass of the earth, or any green thing, or any tree, but only those men who do not have the seal of God on their foreheads. And they were not given authority to kill them, but to torment them for five months. Their torment was like the torment of a scorpion when it strikes a man. In those days men will seek death and will not find it; they will desire to die, and death will flee from them.*

The shape of the locusts was like horses prepared for battle. On their heads were crowns of something like gold, and their faces were like the faces of men. They had hair like women's hair, and their teeth were like lions' teeth. And they had breastplates like breastplates of iron, and the sound of their wings was like the sound of chariots with many horses running into battle. They had tails like scorpions, and there were stings in their tails. Their power was to hurt men five months. And they had as king over them the angel of the bottomless pit, whose name in Hebrew is Abaddon, but in Greek he has the name Apollyon.
Revelation 9:1-11, NKJV

"Abaddon" in Hebrew and "Apollyon" in Greek both mean a demonic personality that destroys! Here are dark forces whose purpose is to confuse humanity so that mankind makes choices that undo their lives.

It is interesting that this verse reference is 9/11! This verse is a part of the first "woe" to come upon the earth. The vision is cryptic, with scorpions, locusts and other symbols of nature wreaking havoc on the earth.

A more in-depth look at these words seems to imply that these strange creatures coming out of the bottomless abyss are inflicting their pain by causing confusion and wrong choices.

The word "scorpion" comes from the root word "skeptomas" from which our English word "skeptic" is derived. It means to question and scrutinize the truth. These scorpions poison humanity with lies that create wrong decisions that bring pain.

The word "locust", which is translated from the word "akrides" in Greek, comes from the root word "akmen" which means "to argue and make a point." It means also to consume another with overwhelming arguments (similar to the way a swarm of locusts overwhelms).

The grass referred to in Revelation 9:11 represents human beings.

. . . but the rich in his humiliation, because as a flower of the field he will pass away.
James 1:10

All flesh is as grass,
And all the glory of man as the flower of the grass.
The grass withers,
And its flower falls away . . .
1 Peter 1:24

In the last days humanity will be invaded by demons who will inflict pain through the scorpions of skepticism and locust of propaganda. This will consume men and cause them great harm.

I believe that the pit is open and the demons of deception are hard at work. This scene is a New Testament picture of Hosea's warning.

My people are destroyed for lack of knowledge.
Because you have rejected knowledge,
I also will reject you from being priest for Me;
Because you have forgotten the law of your God,
I also will forget your children.
Hosea 4:6

Demonic attacks always begin with undermined truth. The attack on the truth is intense today and it is important that we be equipped to take down the lies that are destroying our homes, churches and nation.

As we pull back the curtain and reveal the truth throughout the pages of this book, you will discover some of the lethal effects of Apollyon, the demon controlling the direction of our nation.

For example:

• For the first time states are legalizing brain destroying drugs!

• There is continuing pressure to normalize homosexual activity, even calling it marriage. This goes on while the traditional American family is constantly undermined by the radical left.

• There is the immoral confiscation of the wealth of hard working people through unjust taxes and fees.

• There is the replacement of accurate, honest news with propaganda. Case in point, in 2012, our government stood by while our property in Benghazi experienced a premeditated attack by Islamic terrorists killing our ambassador and his brave defenders. Our fumbling leadership has lied about the attack and have not been held responsible. The murdering terrorists are yet to answer for this act of war.

• There is scandal, cover up and abuse of power in the IRS.

• There is an attack on the Judeo-Christian heritage of America, signaling a godless takeover of government, education and the public square.

• Freedom of religion is now freedom from religion. The Bible has been abandoned, prayers are forbidden, Christian symbols are being insulted, and the Christian population is being ignored.

• America's religious heritage is being attacked while death dealing Islam is given a pass! Foreign policy is the policy of apology and appeasement. Our enemies no longer fear us and our friends no longer trust us. America is waffling over its support of our only ally in the Middle East – Israel.

• The steady slaughter of the unborn continues in hospitals and abortion clinics across the nation.

• News and entertainment media promote occult, immoral, and anti-American values.

BUT THERE IS HOPE FOR AMERICA!

Yes, we have been invaded, but not by an army of men with modern weapons. We have been invaded by spiritual forces that are at work at this very hour, chipping away - bit by bit - at the very underpinnings of this nation that was founded on the Judeo-Christian heritage.

King David said in Psalm 11:3, *"If the foundations are destroyed, what can the righteous do?"*

Never in our nation's history have David's words been more true than they are today! Where are God's people in all of this? I am afraid the church is losing its prophetic voice. Many in the church are substituting popular culture for true faith, comfort zones for battle strategies, moral relativism for decent standards, self-improvement for the cross, and dead works for the Holy Spirit's power!

My prayer is that this book will offer hope to America. I am not writing from a Democratic or Republican point of view. On the contrary, I am writing from the only viewpoint that makes sense to me: a scriptural point of view. Yes, God has written about all of these things in His Word. It is up to us to search out and separate fact from fiction, and truth from lies.

If I am completely honest with you, you need to know I did not want to write this book. It will make most people angry at some point. It won't make me more popular and this book will not receive a literary award. This book will, however, go down as a record that I was not silent about the moral decline of my day. It will pierce the darkness. It will pull back the curtain and expose those who are pulling the strings and unraveling the fabric of America. This book will give you truth and knowledge of our past, present and hope for the future. You must not stop reading the pages of this book until you get to the end. I believe our greatest days are ahead, not behind us. It may be dark now, but in times of darkness, when truth is abandoned, when faith is forsaken, and when the future looks dim,

God comes with this cry -

Do not be afraid; I am the First and the Last. I am He who lives, and was dead, and behold, I am alive forevermore. Amen. And I have the keys of Hades and of Death.

Revelation 1:17-18, NKJV

Until the church stops fighting itself and turns its attention to those spreading the lies that are poisoning and tearing our nation apart, you can be sure that the forces of hell, including radical Islam, will not stop their advance . It is time for the followers of Christ to stop using ignorance as an excuse. God does not want us to remain in the dark, but walk in the light of truth.

Hosea issued a warning:

My people are destroyed for lack of knowledge. Because you have rejected knowledge, I also will reject you from being priest for Me; Because you have forgotten the law of your God, I also will forget your children.

Hosea 4:6, NKJV

Jesus also emphasized the importance of being alert:

"But take heed to yourselves, lest your hearts be weighed down with carousing, drunkenness, and cares of this life, and that Day come on you unexpectedly.

Luke 21:34, NKJV

Our victory was secured at the cross and empty tomb. You and I do not have to live in the wasteland of lies, or be shackled by hopelessness that nothing will ever change. We will never see a moral and spiritual revolution, nor will we stop the erosion of our own culture unless we prepare for spiritual war. Empowered by the Holy Spirit and armed with the truth of God's Word, the victory is ours – but we must be willing to fight for it!

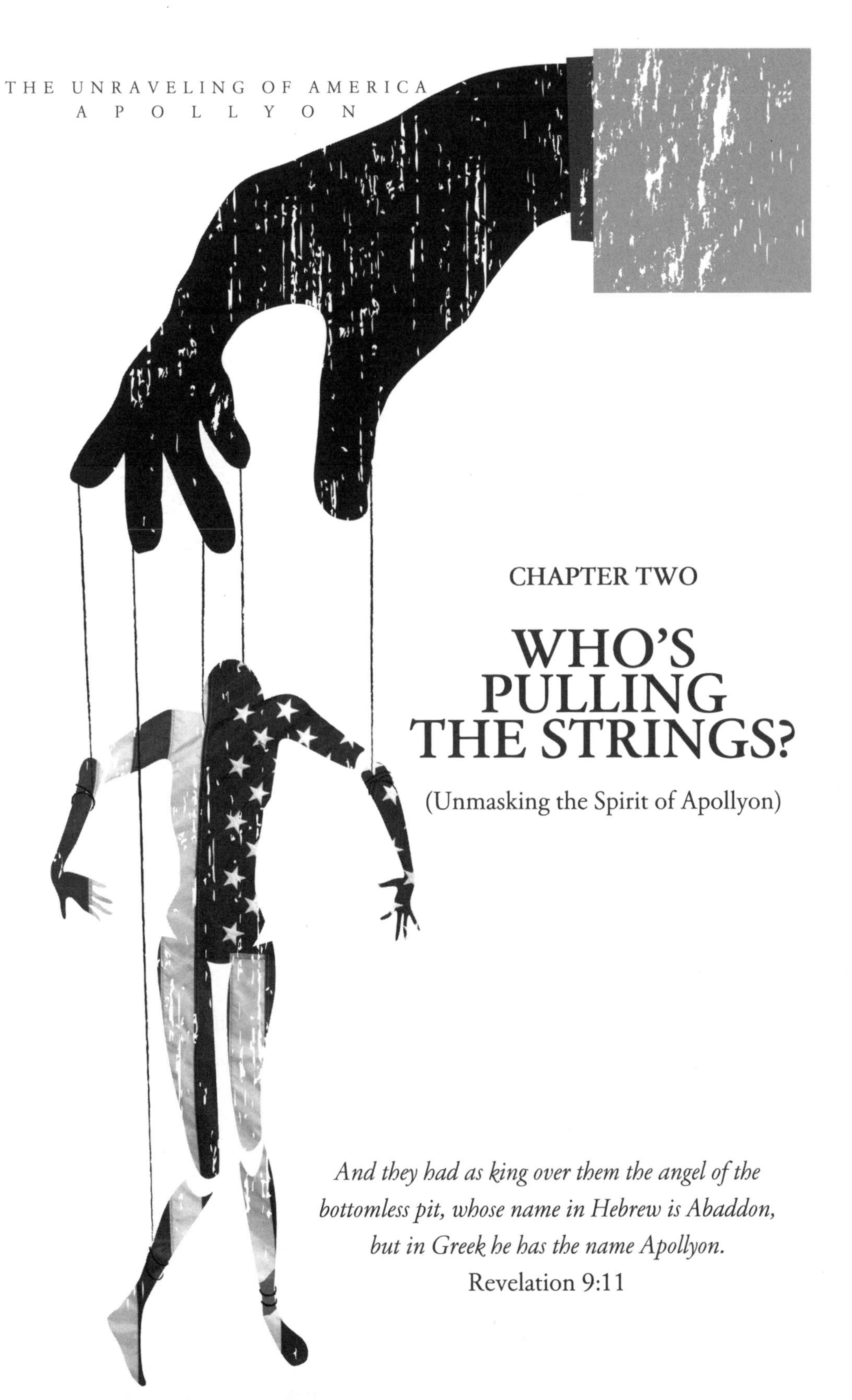

CHAPTER TWO

WHO'S PULLING THE STRINGS?

(Unmasking the Spirit of Apollyon)

And they had as king over them the angel of the bottomless pit, whose name in Hebrew is Abaddon, but in Greek he has the name Apollyon.
Revelation 9:11

Have you ever had the feeling that something is not right, but you just could not put your finger on it? Have you listened to the news and walked away thinking our world has gone mad? If so, you are not alone. Things aren't always as they seem to be. I love to discover the meaning of words and word phrases, so when I study the Bible, I always go back to the original languages - Greek and Hebrew - to discover what each word really means. It is amazing what you will find hidden behind the obvious meaning. So, I decided that the phrase "Who's Pulling the Strings" is the best way to describe what I see happening in our culture. You see, the genesis of the phrase may not be exactly what you thought it was. *"Behind the scenes influence"* is the real meaning of the phrase, and it comes from a popular kid's show in early French culture.

Marionettes are puppets controlled by strings and were popular at the courts of the French monarchy. The puppet shows satirized gossip and could be embarrassing to anyone involved in scandal. When money was slipped to the puppeteer to keep him quiet, or to influence him to embarrass someone else, it was said that the person offering the bribe, and not the puppeteer, was the one pulling the strings of the marionette. The use of behind the scenes influence is often called "pulling strings".[1]

The question we have to ask is: "Who's pulling the strings in our culture?" My answer may not suit your preconception or fit into your ideological box. I am not interested in agendas, political persuasion or being politically correct. I am devoted to the truth, wherever that truth may lead me. The source of all truth is the infallible Word of God, therefore I choose to turn to its pages to find wisdom and insight for what I see and hear around me. Many years ago I came to the conclusion that no matter how sincere people may sound, if it does not line up with the Word it is not truth. Being sincere may be an admirable trait, but sincerity does not always equal truth.

God's purpose is to confront our minds with His truth. He changes our lives and directs us as we respond to His infallible Word. It is the purpose of Satan to confront man's mind with error; the ultimate goal being to enslave. Jesus confirmed the source of lies when He said Satan is a liar and the father of lies: *"You are of your father the devil, and the desires of your father you want to do. He was a murderer from the beginning, and does not stand in the truth, because there is no truth in him. When he speaks a lie, he speaks from his own resources, for he is a liar and the father of it"* (John 8:44, NKJV).

The Bible is very clear in giving important details about the coming Antichrist. We know, according to Scripture, the Antichrist will be a human being given over to Satan. We also know he will be a prominent political figure. Daniel 8:20-22 and 11:40-41 seem to indicate that he will arise out of Media-Persia (which could be our modern Iraq or Iran) or Greece. The Antichrist will declare himself to be God. He will blaspheme all gods, including the demon god Allah, and Jehovah, the true and living God. He is controlled by and worships Satan. He is a deceiver and will convince the religious world into believing his Satanic designs which are hidden from view. 2 Thessalonians 2:1-12 warns us he is the son of perdition, the devil incarnate.

Yet, with that said, I do not believe the Antichrist has, as of yet, been revealed. Of course, in every generation there are Christians who want to point to one particular man as being "the Antichrist." From Nero to Hitler to Osama bin Laden, nearly every evil leader who has emerged on the world stage has been tagged as "the one." As I have already pointed out, the danger lies in looking for a certain individual while ignoring the "spirit of Antichrist" already at work, pulling the strings to influence decisions that are being made on every level of politics, education, media and religion. It is counter-productive to play the name game.

I've come to the conclusion that the spirit of Apollyon is the spirit of Antichrist, working behind the scenes to "influence" thinking patterns that affect us every single day. This demonic spirit is working to set the stage for the revelation of the ultimate man of sin and son of perdition. For those who walk in the light of the truth of God's Word, we must be zealous and fearless to confront error wherever it appears. Tragically, those who are caught in the web of lies often do not see it. We must wake up and realize this is a battleground, not a playground! It's time to unmask the demonic influence poisoning our culture.

The spirit of Antichrist denies the deity of Christ and stands against everything Christians believe. It breeds lawlessness and the breakdown of society. It couches its deception under many different headings. Whether it is called secular humanism, social justice or any other form of progressive liberalism - whatever name you use - it is still the same spirit of error that is blinding men's minds. I am not suggesting that open and honest debate doesn't have its place in a free society. It does. But, I am afraid we have gone beyond that, whereas, if you choose to speak the truth you are labeled a "hater" and "bigot."

Dressing up a pig and calling it by a different name does not change its nature. You can be sure the pig will always find a mud hole to wallow in at the first opportunity. No matter how you "dress up" the spirit of error it will always find a mud hole of deceit and death.

James 5:19-20 warns us what error will do. Error leads to death! *Brethren, if anyone among you wanders from the truth, and someone turns him back, let him know that he who turns a sinner from the error of his way will save a soul from death and cover a multitude of sins.*

Who Is Apollo? (Apollyon)

You might be wondering why you should be concerned with this ancient god. Surely, it has no relevance in our world today, right? Wrong! It has everything to do with our culture, and the decisions that are being made on our behalf. You see, understanding Apollyon is more than learning about a Greek god that can be studied in any college history class. It's about having the understanding that what was prophesied in Scripture is coming to pass right before our very eyes.

The History of the Destroyer

The name Apollyon can be translated as "destroyer." Apollyon was the same name of the god of the Sun known to the Greeks as Apollo or Apollyon. The god Apollo acted as the destroyer of evil, but he was also a bringer of doom. He was also known as the god of purification, who sees and hears all things because he was associated with the sun.

"Apollo was also known as a god of prophecy, as many would bring their sacrifices to him at his temple at Delphi to have their oracle read. The Greeks received oracles from Apollo at Delphi for matters of daily life, and also for military purposes as well.

The practice of offering sacrifices to Apollo lasted well into the third century, and in some places the cult of Apollo lasted until the 6th century CE. It was also known that Apollo had a holy day each seventh day of the month. The seventh day of each month is holy to Apollon, and, of course, the same tradition is used in the christian calendar where the 7th day is named after the sun [Sunday] and is considered holy, and as a day of rest.

In Greek myth, Apollo was the son of Zeus, a sky-god and the Twin of Artemis, goddess of the hunt and of the moon. Just like Artemis, he carried a bow and arrow which he used to cause destruction. As the goddess Athena watched over Apollon at the battle of Troy, she titled Apollon as the Striker From Afar. This is similar to John's writing that tells how Apollyon is from a bottomless pit of destruction. Apollo was known as the twin of Artemis and he had also been referred to as the Striker from Afar (Hymn to Apollon)."[2]

The Apollo Effect

Lest you think Apollo was nothing more than an ancient god depicted and glorified in Homers Iliad or worshipped in ancient Greece, think again. I am not suggesting that suddenly the entire Western population will re-ignite the overt worship of Apollo, or that we will see new temples erected and dedicated to this mythical god. The truth is far more subtle than that. The "Apollo effect" is a system of influence, an underlying strategy to move our culture to the tipping point of accepting an eventual world leader who will be able to bring order out of chaos, a chaos which the spirit of Antichrist created!

But, I do find it interesting that there is a revival of pagan worship in parts of the world in a time we thought such things were buried in ancient history.

Helena Smith, writing in the Guardian, states: "For years, Orthodox clerics believed that they had defeated Greeks wishing to embrace the customs and beliefs of the ancient past. But increasingly the church, a bastion of conservatism and traditionalism, has been confronted by the specter of polytheists making a comeback in the land of the gods. Last year, the group Ellinais, succeeded in gaining legal recognition as a cultural association in a country where all non-Christian religions, bar Islam and Judaism, are prohibited. As a result of the ruling, which devotees say paves the way for the Greek gods to be worshipped openly, the organization hopes to win government approval for a temple in Athens where pagan baptisms, marriages and funerals could be performed."[3]

In answering the question, "What ever happened to the Greek and Roman gods?" Author Hannah M. G. Shapero writes: "So here's yet another answer to whether anyone still worships the old Olympian gods: yes! They may not be "original" believers – they're most likely computer programmers living near large American cities – but they are sincere. Not only do they believe that the old gods exist, they believe that Zeus, Apollo, or other Roman or Greek deities can answer prayers, give prophetic dreams, comfort the worshipper in affliction, bring good fortune, or even heal illnesses. They don't have the elaborate temple structure and priesthood that the ancient religion had – their numbers and resources are far too small for that. But these neo-Olympians will build little shrines and personal altars, at which they burn candles and incense, and offer simple gifts like small cakes and flowers, much as the ancients did at their own niches. Yes, ancient worship lives again."[4]

On February 15, 2014, CNN released the following statement concerning the fisherman who pulled a statue of Apollo from the waters off the coast of Gaza:

When Jwdat Abu Ghrb spotted a dark shape last summer in the waters off Gaza, where he was diving for fish, he initially thought it was a corpse. "I was afraid," he told CNN. "I put on my goggles, dove underneath and still couldn't tell what it was. I resurfaced and got some help from other people and family members and came back, and after a full four hours of trying we managed to get it out of the water and I was shocked by what I found." It was a life-size bronze statue, believed to be a 2,500-year-old depiction of the ancient Greek god Apollo. He described the half-ton object as "treasure pulled out of the sea."[5]

Does it seem odd to you that suddenly a statue of Apollo, which has been under water for centuries comes into view and is pulled out of the water off the coast of Gaza? It may be another sign that the times and seasons are letting us know that an acceleration of prophecy is commencing.

The Apollo Effect In the New Testament

The public worship of Apollo in the Mediterranean was in direct competition with Christianity during the time that John wrote Revelation. The use of the name Apollyon within the Bible, as the 'Angel of the Pit' was a direct association with this Greek god Apollo as Satan, an adversary to Christianity.

Author Thomas Horn gives more insight into the influence of Apollo in the New Testament:

"Another interesting example of spiritual insight by an Apollonian Sibyl is found in the New Testament Book of Acts. Here the demonic resource that energized the Sibyls is revealed (The sibyls were women that the ancient Greeks believed were oracles, prophetesses inspired by demon gods.)

> *And it came to pass, as we went to prayer, a certain damsel possessed with a spirit of divination [of python, a seeress of Delphi] met us, which brought her masters much gain by soothsaying: The same followed Paul and us, and cried, saying, These men are the servants of the most high God, which shew unto us the way of salvation. And this did she many days. But Paul, being grieved, turned and said to the spirit, I command thee in the name of Jesus Christ to come out of her. And he came out the same hour. And when her masters saw that the hope of their gains was gone, they caught Paul and Silas... And brought them to the magistrates, saying, These men, being Jews, do exceedingly trouble our city.*
> Acts 16:16-20

The story in Acts is interesting because it illustrates the level of culture and economy that had been built around the oracle worship of Apollo. It cost the average Athenian more than two days' wages for an oracular inquiry, and the average cost to a lawmaker or military official seeking important state information was ten times that rate. This is why, in some ways, the action of the woman in the book of Acts is difficult to understand. She undoubtedly grasped the damage Paul's preaching could do to her industry. Furthermore, the Pythia of Delphi had a historically unfriendly relationship with the Jews and was considered a pawn of demonic power.[6]

The Apollo Effect in Physics and Science

Have you heard of CERN? If the answer is no, don't feel bad, most people haven't. Only the well informed physicist and mathematician would have any idea of the research that is currently going at CERN headquarters near Geneva, Switzerland.

Standing outside of their main headquarters is the Hindu god of destruction, Shiva, a gift from the government of India. This should give you some idea that this is no ordinary research facility.

"CERN is the European Organization for Nuclear Research. The name CERN is derived from the acronym for the French Conseil Européen pour la Recherche Nucléaire, a provisional body founded in 1952 with the mandate of establishing a world-class fundamental physics research organization in Europe. At that time, pure physics research concentrated on understanding the inside of the atom, hence the word 'nuclear'. Its business is fundamental physics: finding out what the universe is made of and how it works.

Complex scientific instruments are used at CERN to study the basic constituents of matter — the fundamental particles. By studying what happens when these particles collide, physicists learn about the laws of Nature. The instruments used at CERN are particle accelerators and detectors. Accelerators boost beams of particles to high energies before they are made to collide with each other or with stationary targets. Detectors observe and record the results of these collisions. The CERN Laboratory sits astride the Franco–Swiss border near Geneva. It was one of Europe's first joint ventures and now has 20 Member States."[7]

If you have heard me preach for any length of time, you are aware of my love for science. Many experts in the sciences believe the complex work being done at CERN could have Biblical implications. Keep John's Revelation and Paul's statement in Colossians in mind as you consider what I am about to share with you.

Then the fifth angel sounded: And I saw a star fallen from heaven to the earth. To him was given the key to the bottomless pit. And he opened the bottomless pit, and smoke arose out of the pit like the smoke of a great furnace. So the sun and the air were darkened because of the smoke of the pit.
Revelation 9:1-2

For by Him all things were created that are in heaven and that are on earth, visible and invisible, whether thrones or dominions or principalities or powers. All things were created through Him and for Him. And He is before all things, and in Him all things consist.
Colossians 1:16-17

Located at CERN headquarters in Switzerland is a machine more powerful than anything the world has ever seen, the Large Hadron Collider or the LHC. This powerful particle accelerator spans 17 miles, and is, by far, the most powerful particle accelerator ever made. The work being done at CERN is pure science, however, it is not without controversy, drawing strong opinions from proponents and opponents alike. An internet search on the LHC will produce articles with a different opinion from story to story. Many physicists believe that what is taking place there has the potential to destroy not just the world, but the entire universe. You may think such an event could never happen, and is quiet unimaginable. Regardless of what we may think, what they are trying to do is not without colossal risk.

Professor Stephen Hawking, considered by many as one of the most brilliant minds of our generation, has sparked controversy with his comments about the LHC and what it might discover. It is reported that he believes it "…could pose grave dangers to our planet…the God Particle (also known as the Higgs Boson Particle) found by CERN could destroy the universe." Hawking goes on to say… "that the Large Hadron Collider is generating such unbelievable amounts of energy that there is a danger it could inadvertently create a 'vacuum bubble.' Essentially he is saying that because the universe is fundamentally unstable, in discovering the Higgs Boson, such tremendous energy is released that space and time itself can collapse catastrophically through something called "vacuum decay." Hawking has even suggested that the LHC and what they are doing there actually "scares him."[8]

What could they be trying to achieve?

- Re-create the Big Bang
- Discover and create Dark Matter
- Discover and produce quarks and stranglets
- Create powerful high-energy collisions to produce the conditions necessary to bring about time travel

But, there is more.

Former CERN Director General, Rolf-Dieter Heuer, who is also Director of Research at CERN, gave an interview to the British press in which he said that one of the key overall aims of the LHC is to open a "portal to another dimension." This would explain why they are so determined to recreate the conditions of the "Big Bang."

In his comments, General Heuer stated his reasons for wanting to open this portal as follows, "...When we open the door, something might come through it into our reality! Or, we might send something through it into their reality!" Sergio Bertolucci, Director of Research and Scientific Computing at CERN, mirrored General Heuer's statements almost identically in a briefing to reporters at CERN HQ in September 2009, "Out of this door might come something, or we might send something through it."[9]

There is so much more to this story, but I challenge you to research this for yourself. Don't just take my word for it. There are things going on behind the scenes that most people do not know about, but are finally being brought into the light of scrutiny. Who is pulling the strings? I believe that both the Bible and science give us unmistakable proof that Jesus Christ is holding the universe together, and if He were to relax his grip, every atom in the universe would split and be destroyed by fire.

> *For by Him all things were created that are in heaven and that are on earth, visible and invisible, whether thrones or dominions or principalities or powers. All things were created through Him and for Him. And He is before all things, and in Him all things consist.*
> Colossians 1:16-17

> *But the day of the Lord will come as a thief in the night, in which the heavens will pass away with a great noise, and the elements will melt with fervent heat; both the earth and the works that are in it will be burned up. Therefore, since all these things will be dissolved, what manner of persons ought you to be in holy conduct and godliness.*
> 2 Peter 3:10-11

Could it be the scientists might inadvertently open a portal or a door, not to another dimension, but into the spiritual realm; perhaps even to the bottomless pit itself? I do not believe these scientists have any idea how utterly dangerous these experiments can be! Do these discoveries at CERN give more verifiable proof of the biblical account of creation, not to mention the ultimate authority and creative power of God? I believe they do.

The Apollo Effect in Washington DC

You may be shocked to know that in our own nation, at the very center of power and authority, Washington D.C. is covered in pagan and occult symbols. When one stops to consider the ramifications of such a discovery it staggers the mind. You may think I am a conspiracy theorist, and if that be the case you would be wrong. A few simple keystrokes on a computer might convince you that what I'm saying is not conspiracy, but fact. Please understand that I am not suggesting the founding fathers - Jefferson, Adams, Madison, etc. - were devil worshippers. However, I am suggesting that the foundation of the most powerful city on the planet is adorned with interesting details that most Americans know nothing about.

Consider just a few of the many unanswered questions:

• Why are the US government buildings (United States Capitol building, state capitol buildings, court buildings, libraries, and national banks) modeled after pagan Greek and Roman architecture?

• Why does the Lincoln Memorial reflect the design of the Parthenon, which is a religious Greek temple dedicated to the goddess Athena?

• Why do we find on the top of the U.S. Capitol building the pagan statue of Freedom? If you look closely you will see the twelve stars around the headdress of the Statue of Freedom which represents the Zodiac, an ancient Pagan astrological concept.

• Why do our currency symbols reflect pagan gods and goddesses with references to the goddess of Liberty, goddess of Justice, Minerva, and Hercules? Why is it that none of the early American currency used the motto "In God We Trust?"

Apollo will even welcome you to the Library of Congress! Author and researcher James Veverka writes, "With regularity we see America portrayed as the Roman Goddess Minerva. She is victorious in war and she represents wisdom and intellectual pursuits in peacetime. There are scores of pagan Gods and Goddesses in government buildings but not one representation of Jesus. That would be odd for any nation supposedly founded on the Christian religion. In the revolutionary days of America, which coincided with the Enlightenment and a neoclassical revival, Christian themes or figures were not used much in allegorical fashion to represent liberty or America."

He continues on to say Apollo and the Muses are displayed in an obvious matter inside of the Library of Congress, "Apollo, the son of

Zeus, was the guardian of the nine Muses, also daughters of Zeus. In the paintings of the Library of Congress, Apollo represents light, literature, and knowledge; enlightenment. His half-sisters are also on hand in the library to represent the different aspects of literature and song, epic and lyric poetry.

Calliope was the head Muse of Epic Poetry among the nine Muses. Her symbols include a writing tablet, stylus, a lyre and a laurel crown. As the patron of epic poetry, she had a beautiful voice and was called "fair voiced". She stood for truth.

But it is Apollo, Sun God of light, literature and wisdom, who protects the muses of music and poetry. Riding across the skies is Apollo guiding his chariot. Seen with what looks a lot like the Muses is another painting of Apollo as Literature."[10]

Is it possible that the foundation of this nation, as well as the majority of Western culture, has a mixture poured into its formation that will eventually be used to undermine and corrupt its very values and ideals? For me, the answer is yes. It has been the strategy of the antichrist spirit all along. Why do you think we have seen an increase in the moral and spiritual decay in this nation?

The Apollo Effect and Secret Societies

Secret societies are typically groups whose rituals and activities are hidden away from non-members. Since the time of the crusades, hundreds of secret societies have been formed from different parts of the world to serve diverse political, social and religious purposes. Many are no longer active. Some of them are familiar and some are not, but to say that our country has not had its share would be a falsehood. Secret societies have been a part of the American fabric since its inception.

Here is a short list of the most popular:

1. Skull and Bones
2. The Illuminati
3. The Bilderberg Group

4. Rosicrucian's
5. Freemasons

By all accounts, the Skull and Bones secret society at Yale University is the most well-known of all secret societies mainly because of its connection to America's highest office and the allegations that hundreds of our nation's top leaders are or have been members. This secret society was formed by a small group of senior students in 1832 to show their resistance to the debating societies of the University.

Republicans and Democrats were both members of what has been called "an elite secret society only known to the few who are members." When pressed for details about their membership, most decline to share any details. Again, why should we be concerned about a secret society with a small membership at an Eastern establishment university?

Before the 2004 election, 60 Minutes produced an investigative report that shed some light on the matter titled, Skull and Bones: Secret Yale Society Includes America's Power Elite.

It said in part, "Over the years, Bones has included presidents, cabinet officers, spies, Supreme Court justices, captains of industry, and often their sons and lately their daughters, a social and political network like no other. And to a man and woman, they'd responded to questions with utter silence until an enterprising Yale graduate, Alexandra Robbins, managed to penetrate the wall of silence in her book, 'Secrets of the Tomb,' reports CBS News Correspondent Morley Safer. 'I spoke with about 100 members of Skull and Bones and they were members who were tired of the secrecy, and that's why they were willing to talk to me,' says Robbins. 'But probably twice that number hung up on me, harassed me, or threatened me.'

'Skull and Bones is so tiny. That's what makes this staggering,' says Robbins. 'There are only 15 people a year, which means there are about 800 living members at any one time.' But a lot of Bonesmen have gone on to positions of great power, which Robbins says is the main purpose of this secret society: to get as many members as possible into positions of power. 'They do have many individuals in influential positions,' says Robbins. 'And that's why this is something that we need to know about.'"[11]

You may be wondering, "What am I supposed to make of all of this?" Secret societies, exploding atoms, pagan symbols covering Washington DC, and pagan statues being dragged out of the ocean?

I'm simply setting the stage to show you how the antichrist spirit has invaded and permeated culture with its demonic influence.

The apostle John wrote a letter of warning to the people of his day which will give us the advantage amidst the dangerous enemy we face. In 1 John 4:1 he writes, *Beloved, do not believe every spirit, but test the spirits, whether they are of God; because many false prophets have gone out into the world.* We must not be gullible and immature, accepting everything we hear, even when it comes from sources that claim to be Christian. John made it clear that there is a titanic struggle going on between the forces of truth and the forces of evil. We must not be destroyed by a lack of knowledge.

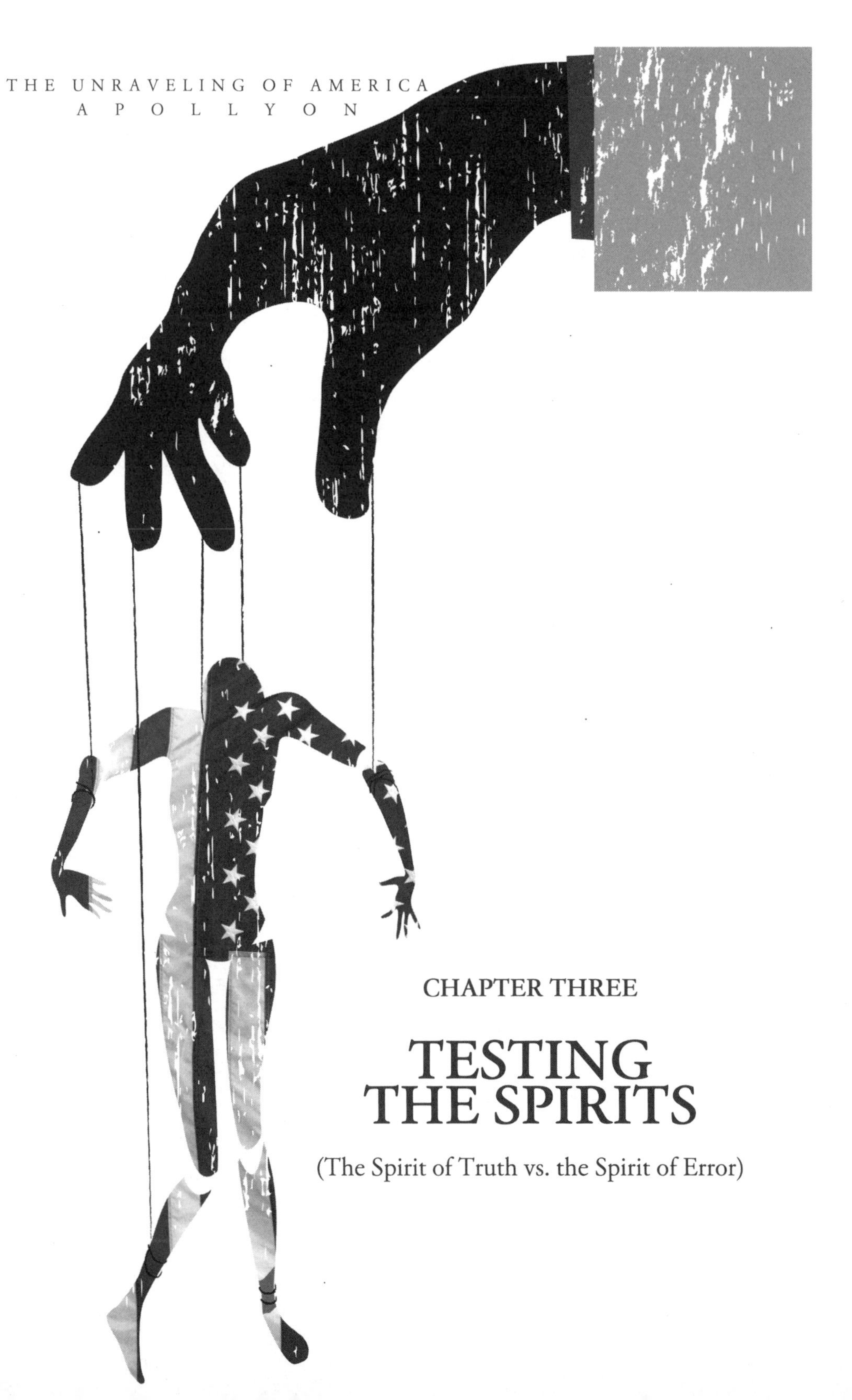

CHAPTER THREE

TESTING THE SPIRITS

(The Spirit of Truth vs. the Spirit of Error)

Beloved, do not believe every spirit, but test the spirits, whether they are of God; because many false prophets have gone out into the world. By this you know the Spirit of God: Every spirit that confesses that Jesus Christ has come in the flesh is of God, and every spirit that does not confess that Jesus Christ has come in the flesh is not of God. And this is the spirit of the Antichrist, which you have heard was coming, and is now already in the world.

You are of God, little children, and have overcome them, because He who is in you is greater than he who is in the world. They are of the world. Therefore they speak as of the world, and the world hears them. We are of God. He who knows God hears us; he who is not of God does not hear us. By this we know the spirit of truth and the spirit of error.
1 John 4:1-6

Christians are some of the most wonderful people, but let's face it, they can also be some of the most gullible. We are living in a time where we have a tendency to believe just about anything as long as it is couched in language that has the slightest hint of "Christian speak." Merriam-Webster gives a very simple definition of the word gullible: "easily fooled or cheated; especially quick to believe something that is not true."[1]

Solomon spoke to the issue of gullibility and naïveté several times in his collection of wisdom called Proverbs. I love the Message translation of Proverbs 14:15, *"The gullible believe anything they're told; the prudent sift and weigh every word."* If we are ever going to be "wise as serpents and harmless as doves" (Matthew 10:16), we must heed the wisdom of Scripture and stop being so naive and gullible.

The old saying, "If it sounds too good to be true, it probably is," should be the motto for us all.

Solomon gives us 3 traps to avoid:

1. Stop being so simple minded.

> *How long, you simple ones, will you love simplicity? For scorners delight in their scorning, and fools hate knowledge.*
> Proverbs 1:22

Most of the men I know would never dream of asking directions, or read an instruction book. It's just beneath our dignity to have to ask. No, we want simplicity, just grab it and go. I am afraid that kind of attitude has crept its way into the Church. We don't want to read the instruction book, the Bible, we just want things to be simple and easy without any deep thought or examination. Accepting things at face value has caused more problems than we can imagine.

2. Stop assuming things will stay the same.

> *Do not boast about tomorrow, for you do not know what a day may bring forth.*
> Proverbs 27:1

Solomon is saying we should not assume things will still be tomorrow the way they are today. Most never believed they would see the rapid unraveling of American culture that we see taking place today. Making quick decisions and shooting from the hip is not the way Solomon would advise anyone to live. Unfortunately, that way of thinking has become the attitude of many believers. Assuming we can make mistakes today and fix them tomorrow will only lead to chaos and confusion.

3. Stop making quick decisions.

The plans of the diligent lead surely to plenty, But those of everyone who is hasty, surely to poverty.
Proverbs 21:5

A popular CNBC television show called "American Greed," tells the sad story of everyday investors who make bad decisions that end up costing millions of dollars. Most of the time, they are taken advantage of by slick, underhanded white collar thieves. These "slick willies" prey on the naïveté of people whose desire to get rich quick overrides their ability to look into the matter thoroughly and make wise decisions. Being pushed into making a quick decision without thorough research will usually lead to heartache and pain.

Solomon's advice was simple. He challenged us to "weigh every word" or "look well into the matter" before making decisions that affect not only our lives, but the lives of those around us.

Somehow, I can't help but believe that the apostle John would agree with Solomon's wisdom. John cautioned us to "not believe every spirit, but test the spirits, whether they are of God." Two totally different men, both writing under the inspiration of the Holy Spirit, telling us to do the same thing. It is time to test every word we hear by the measuring stick of Scripture. If we don't wake up soon, our ideals and values will wither and die. We will end up on the trash heap of history, a footnote at the end of an essay on "The Rise and Fall of America!"

The Spirit of Truth vs the Spirit of Error

Beloved, do not believe every spirit, but test the spirits, whether they are of God; because many false prophets have gone out into the world.
1 John 4:1

John issues a warning that will solidify us against the danger of spiritual naïveté and gullibility. As Christians we must be willing to test those things which we hear and not fall victim to the unseen world where a titanic struggle is taking place for the very minds of men. Behind the world which we perceive with our five senses is an unseen world which is more real than we can imagine. Paul pulls back the curtain on the unseen world in Ephesians 6:12, *"For we do not wrestle against flesh and blood, but against principalities, against powers, against the rulers of the darkness of this age, against spiritual hosts of wickedness in the heavenly places."* There is a spirit of truth which is of God, and there is a spirit of error which is of the evil one. This error is not limited to a certain church, denomination or political party.

Every day we make choices about what we hear. That's why it's so important to apply a spiritual test when things come at us that may sound true, but underneath the surface just don't line up with the truth of God's Word.

John said we must be willing to "try the spirits." The word translated "try" could be translated "test" or "to prove." In John's day, the phrase was used to mean putting metals to the test to see if they were genuine. We might say in our day we need to put things to the "acid test."

Pastor Paul Chappell wrote about the meaning of the phrase "acid test." He stated, "There are a lot of metals that on the surface look similar to gold. Centuries ago, people discovered that unscrupulous operators would take advantage of this to trick people into paying for worthless metal. In order to determine whether gold was genuine or not, scientists devised an "acid test." The item that is supposed to be gold is rubbed on a black stone, leaving a mark behind. Gold is what is called a noble metal, meaning that it is resistant to the corrosive effects of acid. If the mark is washed away by the acid, then the metal is not real gold. If it remains unchanged, the genuine nature of the gold is proven.

It is not always immediately apparent from the outside whether someone is a genuine believer, doing work for God out of good motives or not. Some are tares among the wheat, while others are doing the right things but for selfish motives. It is only when faith and works are put to the test that it will become clear. Not all of these tests will turn out as people expect."[2]

The Apostle Paul echoed the same sentiment in his opening prayer in the letter he wrote to the church at Philippi. He wanted them to know the importance of making right choices and to test things before they acted. The two key words he used were "discernment" and "sincerity."

> *And this I pray, that your love may abound still more and more in knowledge and all discernment, that you may approve the things that are excellent, that you may be sincere and without offense till the day of Christ".*
> Philippians 1:9-10, NKJV

All of our decisions must be guided by discernment, or more literally, sound judgment. This word refers to the practical application of what we learn and what we hear.

The word "sincere" is an interesting one. It has to do with character. In its original meaning the English word "sincere" comes from two Latin words, "sine cera" which means "without wax." The Greek word means "to test by sunshine." In Paul's day, dishonest furniture dealers filled cracks in furniture with wax, and then covered it with shellac, giving the appearance of being genuine when it actually wasn't. Honest furniture dealers would advertise their furniture "sine cera," saying their furniture was genuine, and "without wax."

We should be as we appear to be, especially when God's light shines upon our actions and attitudes. The same is true when making decisions based on what others tell us. We must "shine the light" of God's truth to see if there is any "wax" in what we hear.

While speaking at Westminster Abbey in London, Frederick Lewis Donaldson listed the "Seven Social Sins" of his day. The sermon was given on March 20, 1925, but you would think he was speaking in 2016!

They are:

- Wealth without work
- Pleasure without conscience
- Knowledge without character
- Commerce without morality
- Science without humanity
- Worship without sacrifice
- Politics without principle[3]

Every election cycle, we find ourselves bombarded with men and women claiming certain things about the Christian faith, each candidate trying to appear more Christian than the other. We are not left in the dark, we just need to apply Acts 17:11 which says, *"These were more fair-minded than those in Thessalonica, in that they received the word with all readiness, and searched the Scriptures daily to find out whether these things were so."* We are also told in 1 Thessalonians 5:21 to, *"Test all things; hold fast what is good."*

Before you trust anything, test everything!

Why is that important? John says, because "many false prophets have gone out into the world." Lest you think that was just in John's day, you need to think again. We have no excuse because we are constantly warned in the Bible that false prophets are among us:

For certain men have crept in unnoticed, who long ago were marked out for this condemnation, ungodly men, who turn the grace of our God into lewdness and deny the only Lord God and our Lord Jesus Christ. Jude 1:4

But there were also false prophets among the people, even as there will be false teachers among you, who will secretly bring in destructive heresies, even denying the Lord who bought them, and bring on themselves swift destruction. 2 Peter 2:1

For false christs and false prophets will rise and show great signs and wonders to deceive, if possible, even the elect. Matthew 24:24

Both inside the walls of the church and out in streets, there are false prophets who are seeking to corrupt the truth and enslave the minds of men and women.

How do you put a false prophet to the test?

In Matthew 7:15-20 Jesus gave us this insight, *"Beware of false prophets, who come to you in sheep's clothing, but inwardly they are ravenous wolves. You will know them by their fruits. Do men gather grapes from thornbushes or figs from thistles? Even so, every good tree bears good fruit, but a bad tree bears bad fruit. A good tree cannot bear bad fruit, nor can a bad tree bear good fruit. Every tree that does not bear good fruit is cut down and thrown into the fire. Therefore by their fruits you will know them."*

A false teacher may be found in positions of spiritual authority. Wolves don't usually attack those of their own pack. When they get hungry they prefer sheep!

There are several ways to test things we hear, whether it be in a sermon on Sunday or in a speech on Monday. We can shine the light of God's word and determine if it's the truth of God or not. I think it's about time to become fruit inspectors, don't you?

Let me suggest a four-way test to determine if it's the truth of God or not:

1. Test their words.

By this you know the Spirit of God: Every spirit that confesses that Jesus Christ has come in the flesh is of God, and every spirit that does not confess that Jesus Christ has come in the flesh is not of God and this is the spirit of the Antichrist, which you have heard was coming, and is now already in the world.

1 John 4:2-3

We often think of a false prophet as someone who stands up and denounces Jesus Christ and all Christians. You may identify a false prophet as someone who claims to have all the answers to life's problems outside Biblical teaching. If that were true, all false prophets would be easy to identify, would they not?

Sadly, that is not the case. Often things they say contain an element of truth. This accomplishes a single purpose: They wrap the lie in enough truth for it to be believable. Just because someone says things that contain truth does not mean they speak truth! I have a beautiful wall clock in my house. In my humble opinion the clock has a major design flaw . . . it's loud! It is so loud that I'm surprised that the neighbors across the street cannot hear it. I did the humane thing, I put it to sleep. One day when I could no longer take it, I took the batteries out. It is forever stuck on 11:50. Now that clock is going to give you the correct time...twice a day! Being right twice a day does not mean it's working or telling you the correct time. Just because someone says things that include truth does not mean they are telling you all the truth all the time!

The key question is: What do they believe about Jesus Christ? If they do not confess that Jesus is God, who came in the flesh, they are not of God. What we believe about Jesus Christ is the cornerstone of truth in matters of faith and practical daily living.

Let's apply this test to Islam. Many believe that Islam is the greatest threat to Christianity the world has ever seen. There are some reports indicating it has become the fastest growing religion of the day. If you want to stir up a hornets nest, just say or publish something negative about Islam or Muhammad. The backlash will be swift and the punishment could mean the loss of life. The core value of free speech is not available in the confines of Islam!

Using John's template of truth, it would be instructive to explore exactly what Islam believes about Jesus Christ.

Islam, founded by Muhammad in the early seventh century, claims its purpose is to restore "monotheistic religion" that has been corrupted by Jews and Christians. Islam does acknowledge Jesus, but only as a significant person within their own religious system. They say Jesus was a prophet and an Apostle of God, but deny He is God, or the "Son of God." The Quran teaches that Jesus will indeed come back one day, but as a Muslim, to revive Islam.

From the days of John's writing to this very hour, heresies abound regarding the core belief surrounding Jesus Christ. False prophets will always be "off" concerning His miraculous birth, atoning death and the blessed hope of His return.

I must give a word of warning! We must watch out for the extreme. Just because someone does not agree with your particular theological position does not make them a false prophet. You and I may not agree on the finer points of theology such as when the rapture of the church will take place, the use of spiritual gifts or any number of issues that Godly men have disagreed about for centuries. The fundamentals of the faith are non-negotiable. The rest are good for lively discussion and debate.

2. Test their appeal.

> *They are of the world. Therefore they speak as of the world, and the world hears them.*
> 1 John 4:5

No doubt there are many Bible believing ministers of God who gather people by the thousands in their churches each week to expound on God's word. Mega-churches and mega-ministries are quite common in America, Europe, Central America and other parts of the world. It is not necessarily the size of the crowd, but the content of the message being proclaimed that produces "red flags" to alert the listener that something is fundamentally wrong.

John is not saying that if you are popular you are automatically a false prophet. But it's also true that one of the characteristics of a false teacher is the ability to gather large crowds of people who will believe in the message no matter the content.

Lynette Schaefer writes in, False Prophets, Teachers and Leaders In the Laodicean Age, “It is evident that we are living in times when absolute truth is no longer regarded as the basis for a statement or a lifestyle. Truth is no longer an absolute; it is now a relative term used to suit the whims of many people and their personal opinions, lifestyles or private interpretations. It is no longer, ‘this is a fact that comes from the Bible; therefore, we need to live by it.’ It is now, ‘you have your beliefs and I have mine, so what is good for you is your own truth, but I have mine.’

Biblical truth was once a revered, respected, authoritative foundation for the Church and society in general. People didn't have trouble knowing right from wrong because of these absolutes. Today, we see a worldview where ‘truth’ is whatever your own reality happens to be. As a result, we are reduced to an unhealthy society that is experiencing family problems, violence, immorality, sickness, laxity, materialism, and so on. Of course, there have always been problems in society to some degree; but why does it seem that now, in this day and age, we are dealing with so much chaos in our world?”[4]

One characteristic of a false prophet is their very convincing nature, plausible and smooth with their words. Everything about their makeup is contrived to win popular approval. That is why the Apostle John said, "they are of the world, and therefore the world recognizes and applauds them."

“Pantheists creep into the ministry, but they are generally cunning enough to concede the breadth of their minds beneath Christian phraseology.” - Charles Haddon Spurgeon, Lectures to My Students[5]

While it's true that false prophets make their appeal toward the world, when it comes to the authentic Church, they become hostile and refuse to come under scrutiny of the Word of God. Their approach is to attack anyone who dares to disagree with them.

Over the last half century, we have been shocked and horrified by the tragic circumstances surrounding false prophets, i.e. cult leaders, and their followers. While it's true most false prophets don't lead their rabid followers to drink poison, it's also true that it can happen in extreme cases.

Below are three of the most notorious cult leaders whose influence led to deadly outcomes for their followers, and in some instances, the public at large.

- **Shoko Asahara:** On March 20,1995, members of Aum Shinrikyo, "Supreme Truth", founded by Asahara in the 1980s, released poisonous nerve gas on five crowded subway trains during morning rush hour in Tokyo, killing 13 people and sickening thousands more.
- **Jim Jones:** On November 18, 1978, this self-ordained Christian minister ordered more than 900 followers of The People's Temple to kill themselves as a revolutionary act. The settlement of Jonestown, in the South American nation of Guyana, will be forever linked to this demonically inspired man.
- **David Koresh:** On April 19, 1993, Koresh (Vernon Howell) allowed more than 70 of his Branch Davidian followers, including women and children, to burn to death as a result of a 51 day standoff with federal law enforcement agents. He imposed his will and charm on his followers by claiming to be the messiah. He taught them the end of the world was near, all the while stockpiling massive amounts of weapons. He also fathered multiple children with cult members, and was believed to have had sex with underage girls.

3. Test their attitude toward "material things."

One of the characteristics of a false prophet is their power to strip followers of all their financial resources. In 2 Peter 2:1-3 the Bible says, *"But there were also false prophets among the people, even as there will be false teachers among you, who will secretly bring in destructive heresies, even denying the Lord who bought them, and bring on themselves swift destruction. And many will follow their destructive ways, because of whom the way of truth will be blasphemed. By covetousness they will exploit you with deceptive words; for a long time their judgment has not been idle, and their destruction does not slumber."*

Author and Bible teacher T. Moss in *Secret's of the False Prophet's Fame, Fortune, and Success*: "Like all aspiring entrepreneurs, the false prophet wants celebrity status and financial freedom. They want to receive all the comforts, service, admiration, and revere that a god would receive. The false prophet is well aware of the potential leverages religious leaders can hold by claiming to have divine power. Through false acclamations of receiving a divine calling to preach the word of God, he uses religion as a source of power and then utilizes that power as a resource for acquiring money."[6]

There is no biblical mandate to abstain from having material posessions. I believe that God will always give us His best when we leave the choice up to Him. It is ok to own a nice house or drive a nice car. For too long, some Christians have adopted the philosophy, especially when it comes to their ministers, "Lord, you keep them humble, and we will keep them poor." God is not opposed to you owning material things, but He does warn us of the problems you may face when things own you.

Paul stated the proper attitude toward material possessions when he said to Timothy, *"Command those who are rich in this present age not to be haughty, nor to trust in uncertain riches but in the living God, who gives us richly all things to enjoy" (1 Timothy 6:17).*

4. Test their character.

Jude 4 states that false prophets are *"ungodly men, who turn the grace of our God into lewdness."* Simply put, it means that false prophets will use and abuse the grace of God in order to excuse an ungodly lifestyle. When they get caught in a compromising and/or potentially criminal matter their response is usually something like, "Because I am an anointed man of God and under the grace of God I have the right to my private life, even if you don't agree with it!"

The inference is, "How dare you question my leadership, my lifestyle and what I do with ministry resources. My spending habits are my business, not yours."

Unfortunately, this scenario is repeated time and time again; preachers and politicians say it doesn't matter how they live in private or what they believe in secret as long as they do their job in public. We must wake up and realize that what a man is on the inside will affect how he lives on the outside!

Warren W. Wiersbe relates the following story about the importance of integrity and character: "Will Rogers was known for his laughter, but he also knew how to weep. One day he was entertaining at the Milton H. Berry Institute in Los Angeles, a hospital that specialized in rehabilitating polio victims and people with broken backs and other extreme physical handicaps. Of course, Rogers had everybody laughing, even patients in really bad condition; but then he suddenly left the platform and went to the rest room. Milton Berry followed him to give him a towel; and when he opened the door, he saw Will Rogers leaning against the wall, sobbing like a child. He closed the door, and in a few minutes, Rogers appeared back on the platform, as jovial as before.

If you want to learn what a person is really like, ask three questions: What makes him laugh? What makes him angry? What makes him weep? These are fairly good tests of character that are especially appropriate for Christian leaders. I hear people saying, "We need angry leaders today!" or "The time has come to practice militant Christianity!" Perhaps, but *"the wrath of man does not produce the righteousness of God" (James 1:20).*

What we need today is not anger, but anguish; the kind of anguish that Moses displayed when he broke the two tablets of the law and then climbed the mountain to intercede for his people or that

Jesus displayed when He cleansed the temple and then wept over the city. The difference between anger and anguish is a broken heart. It's easy to get angry, especially at somebody else's sins; but it's not easy to look at sin, our own included, and weep over it."[7]

Let me reiterate, Jesus pointed out the best way to examine a false prophet is to become a fruit inspector. He said, *"by their fruits you will know them" (Matthew 7:20).* One sure way to determine the validity of a man's message is to examine the kind of people that message produces.

According to 2 Peter 2:19, the product of a false prophet is a counterfeit believer: *"While they promise them liberty, they themselves are slaves of corruption; for by whom a person is overcome, by him also he is brought into bondage."*

Silent no more!

Can we sit silent and allow the corruption that is eating away at the foundation of our nation to continue? Should we sit on the side-lines and watch while godless men with their godless lies take us down the road to destruction? Do we allow the fear of being called narrow-minded or a racist to move us away from the Biblical foundation this country was founded on? We cannot. We must not!

I am going to expose some of the most egregious lies that have been perpetrated on the American people. Some of these perversions of truth have been hidden in the shadows so they would not be exposed to the light of God's truths. Jesus said, *"And you shall know the truth, and the truth shall make you free" (John 8:32).* He also said, *"I am the way, the truth, and the life. No one comes to the Father except through Me" (John 14:6).* Pulitzer prize-winning novelist Herbert Agar said, "The truth that makes men free is for the most part the truth which men prefer not to hear." [8]

I could not agree more . . . it's time to pull back the curtain and reveal truth!

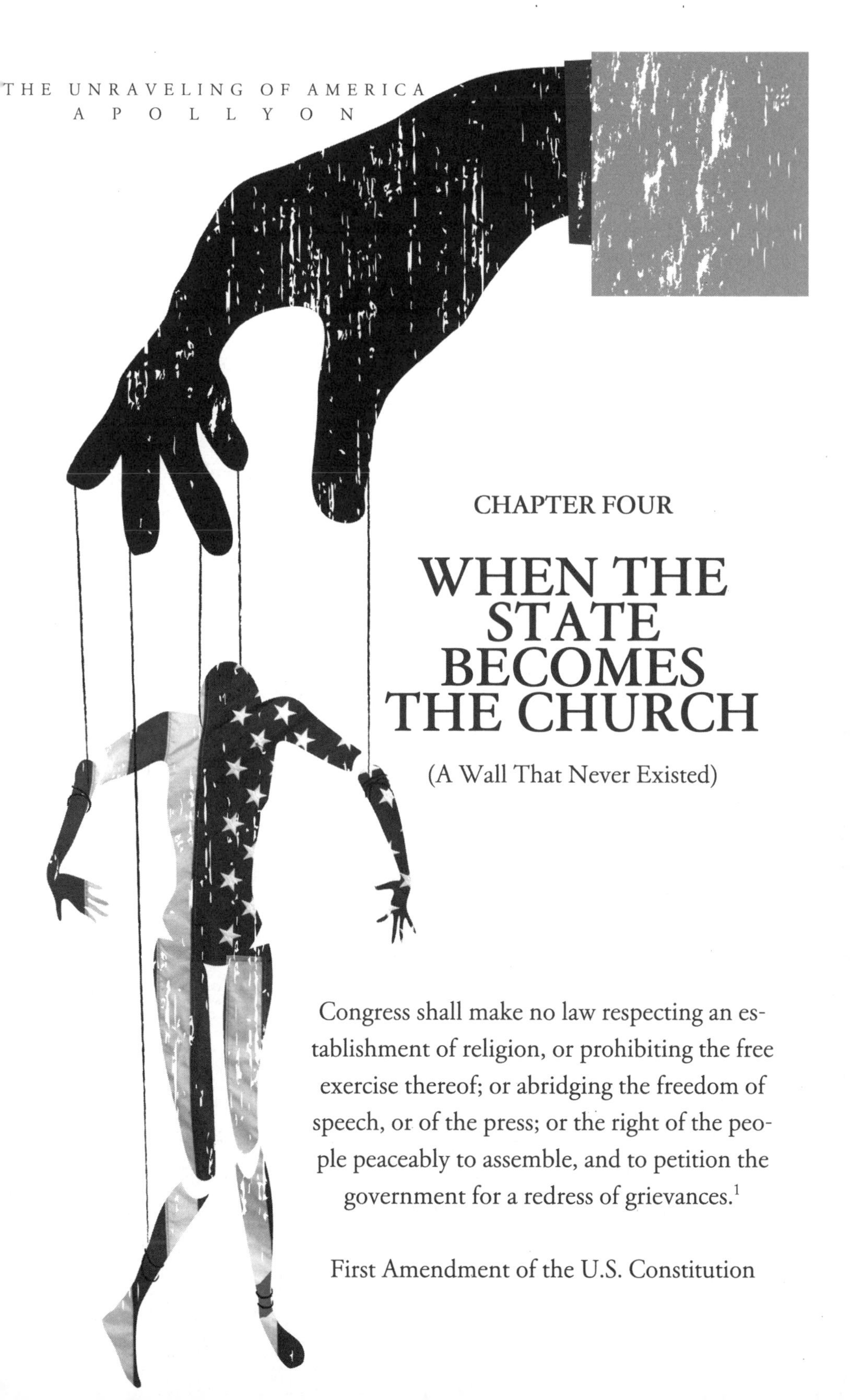

CHAPTER FOUR

WHEN THE STATE BECOMES THE CHURCH

(A Wall That Never Existed)

Congress shall make no law respecting an establishment of religion, or prohibiting the free exercise thereof; or abridging the freedom of speech, or of the press; or the right of the people peaceably to assemble, and to petition the government for a redress of grievances.[1]

First Amendment of the U.S. Constitution

> Had the people, during the (American) Revolution, had a suspicion of any attempt to war against Christianity, that Revolution would have been strangled in its cradle . . . In this age, there can be no substitute for Christianity . . . That was the religion of the founders of the republic and they expected it to remain the religion of their descendants.[2]
> Congress, U. S. House Judiciary Committee, 1854

> *Blessed is the nation whose God is the Lord; and the people whom he hath chosen for his own inheritance.*
> Psalm 33:12

America is in trouble. I remember a time when the Bible was respected as the final template of truth, not only for the churches of America, but also for the society as a whole. From the very birth of our nation, Christian principles guided her and established a worldview unlike any other.

However, while the Christian majority has drifted off to sleep, America has drifted away from our Judeo-Christian moorings. We are experiencing the effect of a planned and concerted effort by demonic forces to destroy the very foundation of this nation, using any means necessary to stop the United States from continuing to be a "light set on a hill" of freedom to the nations.

Because we have "cut ties" with our underpinning, the results are sad and far reaching. Today the general rule is, "Do whatever is right in your own eyes, as long as no one gets hurt in the process." Biblical principles are being pushed overboard to make room for a perversion of truth that was once shunned and condemned for its obvious contradiction to generally accepted Christian and societal standards.

This attitude has led to:

• Accepting the homosexual lifestyle as normal.

• Accepting, without contradiction, the Supreme Court ruling on same-sex marriage.

• A total abandonment of standards in music and entertainment.

• Allowing the demands of Islamist, atheistic and a wide assortment of ungodly practices to infiltrate our educational system.

• Allowing the continuation of infanticide (abortion funded by taxpayer dollars through Planned Parenthood.)

• An increase of random acts of violence such as mass shootings, bombings and other tragic events. This behavior only underscores our society's disdain for time honored qualities of decency and order.

The late Supreme Court Justice, Antonin Scalia spoke at a Catholic school in Metairie, Louisiana, a suburb of New Orleans. The New Orleans Times Picayune reported the following:

Scalia told those gathered at Archbishop Rummel High School that while the First Amendment forbids the government from playing favorites among religions, there is "no place" in U.S. constitutional traditions for the notion that the government must be neutral about religion versus non-religion,"Where did that come from?" he asked.

Scalia added that it wasn't until the 1960s that governmental religious neutrality became the law, when activist judges invoked their own concepts rather than simply taking cues from the American people, the Times-Picayune added.

"Don't cram [prohibition of governmental endorsement of religion] down the throats of an American people that has always honored God," Scalia said, according to the paper. He also said there is "nothing wrong" with the idea of presidents and others invoking God in speeches. He said God has been good to America because Americans have honored him. "I think one of the reasons God has been good to us is that we have done him honor. Unlike the other countries of the world that do not even invoke his name we do him honor. We show honor in presidential addresses, in Thanksgiving proclamations and in many other ways."

"There is nothing wrong with that and do not let anybody tell you that there is anything wrong with that," he added, the AP said.[3]

There was a time when we held the views expressed by our founding fathers as hallowed. Their views were the main ingredient poured into the recipe of a society bound by Christian principles and civil virtues. They allowed for differing opinions and debate, but at the end of the day, they would not allow for a society to be built on any other foundation than the Holy Bible! If it were possible for the likes of Adams, Jefferson, Madison and all signers of the Constitution to view what is happening in our modern culture, they would no doubt be horrified!

There is no disagreement as to what our early leaders thought when it came to the importance of the Christian faith. More contemporary voices have sought to characterize their views as unimportant and ambitious, yet, nothing can be further from the truth. Through the centuries, our nation's leaders have reaffirmed that a civil society must have a solid foundation built on principles and values found in Holy Scripture.

It would be impractical to list all quotes, articles and writings of great American leaders who espoused the principles of the Christian faith and how it related to the birth and continued freedom of our country. Go to the sources listed in the "endnotes" to research these historical facts.

Here is a sampling of the abundant record of the importance of religious faith as it applies to the foundation of our country from a variety of leaders:

- "I conceive we cannot better express ourselves than by humbly supplicating the Supreme Ruler of the world . . . that the confusions that are and have been among the nations may be overruled by the promoting and speedily bringing in the holy and happy period when the kingdoms of our Lord and Savior Jesus Christ may be everywhere established, and the people willingly bow to the scepter of Him who is the Prince of Peace." - Samuel Adams (Signer of the Declaration of Independence; Father of the American Revolution; and ratifier of the U.S. Constitution.)[4]

• "The Bible, when not read in schools, is seldom read in any subsequent period of life... [T]he Bible... should be read in our schools in preference to all other books because it contains the greatest portion of that kind of knowledge which is calculated to produce private and public happiness. - Benjamin Rush (Signer of the Declaration of Independence; Surgeon General of the Continental Army; ratifier of the U.S. Constitution; Father of American medicine; Father of public schools under the Constitution.)[5]

• "In this great country of ours has been demonstrated the fundamental unity of Christianity and democracy." Harry Truman[6]

• "The propitious smiles of Heaven can never be expected on a nation that disregards the eternal rules of order and right, which heaven itself has ordained." George Washington[7]

• "We recognize no sovereign but God, and no King but Jesus!" John Adams[8]

• "The rights of man come not from the generosity of the state but from the hand of God." John F. Kennedy[9]

• "We have forgotten God. We have forgotten the gracious hand, which preserved us in peace and multiplied and enriched and strengthened us, and we have vainly imagined, in the deceitfulness of our hearts, that all these blessings were produced by some superior wisdom and virtue of our own. Intoxicated with unbroken success, we have become too self-sufficient to feel the necessity of redeeming and preserving grace, too proud to pray to the God that made us." Abraham Lincoln[10]

A Wall That Was Never Built

The phrase "separation of church and state" is something I have heard most of my life. Is that statement really contained in the First Amendment of the Constitution? When I read the First Amendment, I cannot find the phrase, or anything like it.

Read it for yourself and see if you come to the same conclusion.

> "Congress shall make no law respecting an establishment of religion, or prohibiting the free exercise thereof; or abridging the freedom of speech, or of the press; or the right of the people peaceably to assemble, and to petition the government for a redress of grievances."

Although the phrase is quite popular, "separation of church and state" is what scholars call an "extra constitutional" statement added in hope of replacing our religious foundation with a more liberal, progressive agenda. It became the first shot fired by the spirit of Antichrist, to separate God from government, and it won't be the last.

How could this have happened? Where did the idea come from that religious values and Christian teaching must be divorced from the public arena, including government and public schools? I agree with David Barton's conclusion that the original intent of the framers of the Constitution was not to eliminate the free exercise of religion in the public square, or in public education. The intent was that Congress would not officially establish any particular denominational influence in America. The original intent was to exclude from Federal endorsement all denominations, without preference or prejudice; including Anglican, Catholic and Baptist. It did not matter to the framers what brand of religion you practiced as long as it was not endorsed as a national denomination by the federal government.

Barton said it well, "Very simply, the founding fathers did not want a single federal denomination to rule America 'Congress shall make no law respecting the establishment of religion…', but they did expect basic biblical principles and values to be present throughout public life and society '… nor prohibiting the free exercise thereof'.

Significantly, for over a century and a half after the First Amendment was ratified, this was the only manner in which it was interpreted. Unfortunately in recent decades activist courts have dramatically redefined the word' religion' in the First Amendment, giving it a definition found in no dictionary (except the Court's own privately written one). The result is that the First Amendment is now used to prohibit the very religious activities that the Founders themselves once encouraged under the same amendment."[11]

George Washington, the nation's first president, gave his farewell address in the form of a letter written to "The People of the United States of America. The purpose of the letter was to inform the public of his desire not to serve another term as President and to issue a warning concerning political dangers that must be avoided if the American populace was to remain true to its values. Included in his "Farewell Address" is his assertion that you cannot separate religion from public life and policy. He cautioned Americans to never reject the notion that morality could be maintained apart from religion.

He stated, "Of all the dispositions and habits which lead to political prosperity, religion and morality are indispensable supports. In vain would that man claim the tribute of patriotism, who should labor to subvert these great pillars of human happiness, these firmest props of the duties of men and citizens. The mere politician, equally with the pious man, ought to respect and to cherish them. A volume could not trace all their connections with private and public felicity. Let it simply be asked: Where is the security for property, for reputation, for life, if the sense of religious obligation desert the oaths which are the instruments of investigation in courts of justice? And let us with caution indulge the supposition that morality can be maintained without religion. Whatever may be conceded to the influence of refined education on minds of peculiar structure, reason and experience both forbid us to expect that national morality can prevail in exclusion of religious principle.

It is substantially true that virtue or morality is a necessary spring of popular government. The rule, indeed, extends with more or less force to every species of free government. Who that is a sincere friend to it can look with indifference upon attempts to shake the foundation of the fabric?"[12]

It is clear from this address and other writings of the founding fathers that they clearly understood that religious teaching and moral values help a free society maintain its common good. Without such a basis of teaching to serve as a firewall against immorality and baseless living, no nation can stand. Once the foundation is destroyed, secular humanism will always fill its space. What started as a slow drip has now become a tidal wave of degeneration crashing on the shores of our religious freedom!

Jefferson, The Danbury Baptist Association and the Wall

The case of the Danbury Baptist Association of Danbury, Connecticut is where the mythical 'wall' began.

Here are the facts:

The Danbury Baptist Association expressed to the newly elected President, Thomas Jefferson, a very real concern over the lack in their state constitution of explicit protection of religious liberty, and against a government establishment of religion. In a letter dated October 7, 1801, they outlined their feeling that a religious majority might "reproach their chief Magistrate... because he will not, dare not assume the prerogatives of Jehovah and make laws to govern the Kingdom of Christ," thus establishing a state religion at the cost of the liberties of religious minorities.

In their letter to the President, the Danbury Baptists affirmed that, "Our Sentiments are uniformly on the side of Religious Liberty": that Religion is at all times and places a matter between God and individuals, that no man ought to suffer in name, person, or effects on account of his religious opinions, [and] that the legitimate power of civil government extends no further than to punish the man who works ill to his neighbor. But sir, our constitution of government is not specific. Our ancient charter, together with the laws made coincident therewith, were adapted as the basis of our government at the time of our revolution. And such has been our laws and usages, and such still are, [so] that Religion is considered as the first object of Legislation, and therefore what religious privileges we enjoy (as a minor part of the State) we enjoy as favors granted, and not as inalienable rights. And these favors we receive at the expense of such degrading acknowledgments, as are inconsistent with the rights of freemen. It is not to be wondered at therefore, if those who seek after power and gain, under the pretense of government and Religion, should reproach their fellow men, [or] should reproach their Chief Magistrate, as an enemy of religion, law, and good order, because he will not, dares not, assume the prerogative of Jehovah and make laws to govern the Kingdom of Christ."[13]

Unlike modern-day politicians who obfuscate to avoid dealing with hard issues, Jefferson met their concerns with the following response:

"Gentlemen,--The affectionate sentiment of esteem and approbation which you are so good as to express towards me, on behalf of the Danbury Baptist Association, give me the highest satisfaction. My duties dictate a faithful and zealous pursuit of the interests of my constituents, and in proportion as they are persuaded of my fidelity to those duties, the discharge of them becomes more and more pleasing.

Believing with you that religion is a matter which lies solely between man and his God, that he owes account to none other for his faith or his worship, that the legislative powers of government reach actions only, and not opinions, I contemplate with sovereign reverence that act of the whole American people which declared that their legislature would "make no law respecting an establishment of religion, or prohibiting the free exercise thereof," thus building a wall of separation between Church and State. Adhering to this expression of the supreme will of the nation in behalf of the rights of conscience, I shall see with sincere satisfaction the progress of those sentiments which tend to restore to man all his natural rights, convinced he has no natural right in opposition to his social duties.

I reciprocate your kind prayers for the protection and blessing of the common Father and Creator of man, and tender you for yourselves and your religious association, assurances of my high respect and esteem. Th Jefferson Jan. 1. 1802"[14]

Thomas Jefferson had no intention of a "wall of separation" being built to eliminate the public display and/or expression of religion, but rather to guarantee security against the government interference with those expressions. Whether it be in the four walls of the church or in the marketplace, he wanted to assure the Baptists of Connecticut (and all others) his firm belief that the singular purpose of the First Amendment was to ensure and declare the government could not, and would not interfere with public expressions of religion.

Each time the Supreme Court had opportunity to rule concerning religious expression, it came down squarely on the view expressed by Thomas Jefferson. They understood that the court, as an extension of the federal government, was not to interfere with religious expression except in a limited category. Only in cases where religious expressions were "in violation of social duties" or "broke out into overt acts against peace and good order,"[15] that the court felt it had a legitimate reason to intrude.

Before our freedoms of religious expression were forever established in the Bill of Rights and the Constitution, the establishment of higher education was founded on the basis of Christian principles.

For Example:

• 1636 - Harvard College is founded by John Harvard, a Presbyterian minister, primarily as a religious school to train clergy in the Christian faith.

• 1642 - Compulsory School law passed in Massachusetts, called the "Old Deluder Satan Law".This law was passed to assure that children could read their Bibles.

• 1693 - Rev. James Blair established William and Mary College to prepare students for the ministry.

• 1701 - Collegiate School, later renamed Yale College, was founded by ten ministers in order to further the reformed Protestant religion. Students were required to read Scriptures morning and evening at times of prayer.

• 1745 - Yale applicants must recite Vigil, the Greek Testament, & bring sufficient testimony of his blameless and inoffensive life.

• 1746 - Princeton was founded by a group of Presbyterians with the Rev. Jonathan Dickinson as its first president. Every student was required to attend worship in the college hall morning and evening at the hours appointed, and to behave with gravity and reverence during the whole service.

• 1764 - Brown University established by the Baptists to further the religious revival known as the "Great Awakening" in America.

• 1769 - Dartmouth-College was established for the education and instruction of youths in reading, writing and all parts of learning which shall appear necessary and expedient for civilizing and Christianizing the children.

• 1787 - Congress passed the Northwest Ordinance which outlined requirements for governments of new territories so they can qualify for statehood. Article 3 of the Northwest Ordinance directed the people of the territories to establish schools "to teach religion, morality, and knowledge." Nearly every state admitted to the Union after this has written in their State Constitution wording that the schools are to teach morality and religion and they all use the Bible as the bases for their teachings.

• 1789 - Georgetown became the first Catholic college in America to serve as a college and seminary to train Roman Catholic clergymen.

Even though the Courts upheld the Jeffersonian view of religious expression each time it was presented an opportunity to rule, the winds of change started blowing in 1947. In a highly celebrated case (Everson v. Board of Education) the Court, for the first time, interpreted the "separation" phrase as requiring the federal government to exclude and to remove religious expression from the public arena. A misinterpretation of eight words from Jefferson's letter to the Danbury Baptist Association forever changed the relationship between the federal government and the religious community.

I propose one of the far-reaching effects of the "wall that was never built" is the exclusion of faith expressions in public education. In the 1958 case, Baer v. Kolmorgen, one of the judges was tired of hearing the phrase and wrote a dissent warning that if the court did not stop talking about "separation of church and state," people were going to start thinking it was part of the Constitution. That warning was in 1958![16]

• 1963 - Supreme Court banned individual school prayer (Murry v. Curlett) and Bible reading in public schools (Abington Township School District v. Schempp).

• 1965 - Supreme Court ruled that a child may pray silently to himself if no one knows he is praying and his lips do not move.

• 1980 - U.S. schools reported the lowest S.A.T. scores ever, after 18 straight years of decline following the 1962 ban on school prayer.

• 1980 - The Supreme Court ruled in the case of Stone v.

Graham, that it was unconstitutional for a student in school to continue, even voluntarily, to see a copy of the Ten Commandments. In a 5-4 decision the court ruled… "the Court found that there was no secular purpose behind the posting of the Ten Commandments. The Commandments are a sacred religious text, and their posting, without any connection to the curriculum, can only be for the purpose of promoting certain religious views."[17]

• 1992 - Supreme Court rules clergy may not offer prayer at graduation ceremonies. (Lee vs. Weisman)

• 1999 - Two students at Littleton, Colorado High School killed eleven students. None of the students had ever seen the Ten Commandments, "Thou shall not kill" in a public school.

• 2000 - Supreme Court ruled student initiated or student led prayer at football games is unconstitutional. (Doe vs. Santa Fe Independent School District)

While the Church is sleeping, America is drifting away from its roots. It is not only liberal courts, but other organizations such as the ACLU that are doing their best behind the scenes, pulling their strings of influence to push our nation over the cliff and into the abyss of a godless America!

One recent and strange example of the upside down world in which we are living involves the case of two Christian schools. Cambridge Christian School and University Christian School, who faced off against each other in the 2A state championship football game, asked the Florida High School Athletic Association if they could begin the game with a word of prayer. The answer came quickly – NO! They were told in no uncertain terms that a pregame prayer was against the law. You see the prayers, according to their logic, would be given on government property (the football field at the school) and would enhance the endorsement of religion.

Remember, we are talking about two Christian schools that were told the teams could not pray before their football game! The schools were represented by the Liberty Institute, which sent a letter to the FHSAA demanding a written apology for what they call a "gross violation" of the law. Should they fail to do so, the law firm has threatened to file a federal lawsuit. The FHSAA has yet to respond to their demands. Not to be intimidated, the teams gathered on the field and recited "The Lord's Prayer" before the game!

Following the tragedy of September 11, 2001, the children at Glenview Elementary School gathered each morning to recite the Pledge of Allegiance. As per tradition, they concluded with "God bless America." But, when the ACLU of New Jersey heard about the practice, they sent a letter to the school's principal informing him that what they were doing was unconstitutional. In a letter to the attorney for the school district, they wrote that the establishment clause of the First Amendment prohibits the government from not only favoring one religion over another, but also from promoting religion over non-religion. The ACLU continued by saying: "The greatest care must be taken to avoid the appearance of governmental endorsement in school, especially elementary schools, given the impressionable age of the children under the schools care and authority."[18]

The school district chose not to fight the ACLU because it lacked the money necessary to do so. So, the fine young boys and girls of Glenview Elementary School cannot start their day with the Pledge of Allegiance ending in "God Bless America." Once again the ACLU struck a blow for the godless, progressive agenda!

When Does the State Become the Church?

- When it begins to regulate what is moral and what is not, therefore replacing the leadership role of the church. It is the church, not the state, that has been given the mandate by God to lead in the moral development of the community.

• When it decides that a legal opinion equals a moral judgment. Think abortion and same-sex marriage.

• When it decides that biblical values are to be replaced by secular humanistic standards in public schools. The removal of the Ten Commandants, prayer and Bible reading are just a few of the examples.

• When churches and ministries are held captive from speaking out against social issues. The "gag order" commonly referred to as a tax exempt status 501c3 in the IRS code is, in effect, shutting the prophetic voice of pastors in the pulpits of America.

• When President Obama visited a fundamentalist mosque in Baltimore on February 3, 2016. The headline of an article about the event sounded eerily familiar: Obama Uses Mosque Speech to Subordinate All Religion to the State.

In his article, Neil Munro writes:

"… He (Obama) used the occasion to flatter his Islamic audience, smiled cheerfully and then rhetorically flattened the constitutional and cultural walls that protect competing religious beliefs from the progressively expanding federal government.

Robert Spencer, an expert on Islamic ideology and best-selling author, says Obama's condescending comments about Islam and all religions reveal his corporatist view of society, in which all elements of society -- religion, industry, unions, family, education -- are subordinated and coordinated by government officials.

For Obama, rival churches are 'just social-work centers, that's all. He doesn't care about the content of doctrine, and pretends they all teach the same things,' Spencer said. Obama is dismissive of rival religious groups' sincere beliefs because 'he doesn't believe that [religious] words mean anything,' Spencer told Breitbart News.

In his most patronizing passage, Obama portrayed 310 million autonomous, free and independent Americans as children under the parental supervision of Uncle Sam. 'We're one American family and when any part of our family starts to feel separate or second-class or targeted, it tears at the very fabric of our nation,' the president claimed, ignoring the nation's long and very successful history of balancing competing ideas and varied lifestyles."[19]

The Antichrist spirit is on the rise and will stop at nothing to eradicate God from the public arena. This spirit's very name reveals its true intent. It is a spirit in direct opposition to Christ, who He is, and what He has done. According to 2 Corinthians 10:4, we have been equipped to overcome the forces of evil. Therefore, we are without excuse!

Every solider knows the hottest part of the battlefield is the ground where the enemy is attacking. Where is he attacking today? It's not just in the churches, but in the halls of power. We see fierce battles over who will be appointed to the Supreme Court when the next vacancy occurs, and who will occupy the White House. Don't be fooled by political correctness and smooth words which would deceive us into believing the 'state' has our best interest at heart. The American church could benefit from a massive dose of spiritual discernment. Who is pulling the strings? This is not a time to bury our heads in the sand and hope it will all go away. It is time to wake up, declare the truth and take a stand.

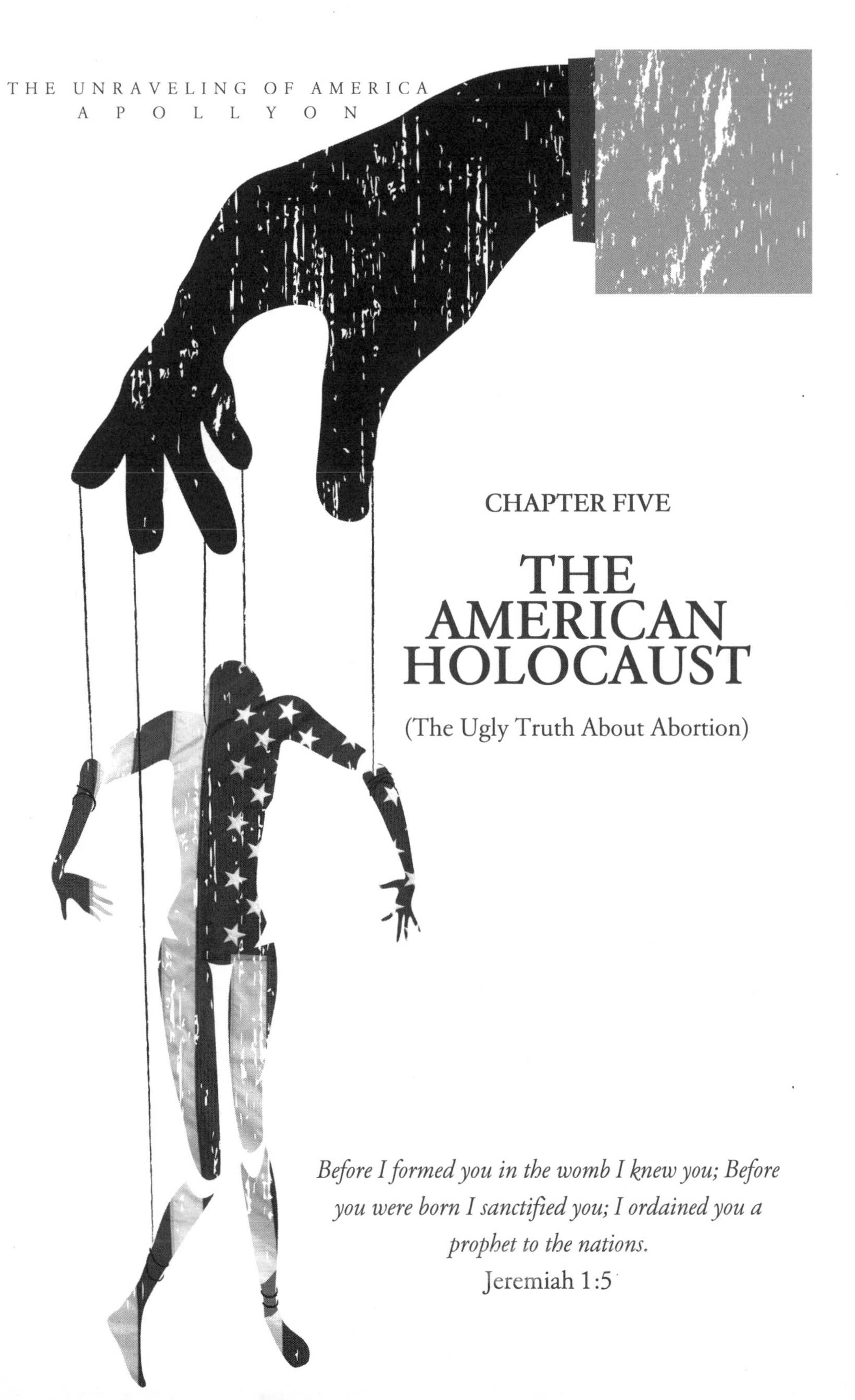

CHAPTER FIVE

THE AMERICAN HOLOCAUST

(The Ugly Truth About Abortion)

Before I formed you in the womb I knew you; Before you were born I sanctified you; I ordained you a prophet to the nations.
Jeremiah 1:5

"More than a decade ago, a Supreme Court decision literally wiped off the books of fifty states statutes protecting the rights of unborn children. Abortion on demand now takes the lives of up to 1.5 million unborn children a year. Human life legislation ending this tragedy will some day pass the Congress, and you and I must never rest until it does. Unless and until it can be proven that the unborn child is not a living entity, then its right to life, liberty, and the pursuit of happiness must be protected."
Ronald Reagan[1]

During the earliest days of the Nazi rule in postwar Germany there emerged a prominent protestant pastor by the name of Martin Niemoller. A quote attributed to him has become a rallying cry against any oppression leveled against those who have no one to speak up for them. The quotation comes from one of his earliest lectures during the postwar period:

First they came for the Socialists, and I did not speak out—
Because I was not a Socialist.
Then they came for the Trade Unionists, and I did not speak out—
Because I was not a Trade Unionist.
Then they came for the Jews, and I did not speak out—
Because I was not a Jew.
Then they came for me—
and there was no one left to speak for me.[2]

It was his firm belief that Christian leaders had been complicit through their silence in the Nazi imprisonment, persecution and murder of millions of people including six million Jews. From the earliest days of Nazi rule, he was one of the few Germans to speak out about the broader complicity in the Holocaust. He paid a heavy price for his courage. Niemoller spent the last seven years of Nazi rule in concentration camps.

In 1963, he gave an interview on West German television. In that interview he acknowledged, with regret, his own anti-Semitism. In his book, published in English in 1946 titled, Of Guilt and Hope, Niemoller wrote: "Thus, whenever I chance to meet a Jew known to me before, then, as a Christian, I cannot but tell him: 'Dear Friend, I stand in front of you, but we cannot get together, for there is guilt between us. I have sinned and my people have sinned against thy people and against thyself.'"[3]

It is almost beyond comprehension to think about how the demonic forces of Nazi Germany tried to eliminate an entire race of people. Only a few courageous voices were willing to speak out against such evil. When the helpless and innocent have no one to speak for them, it always has the potential for evil intent.

Today we are faced with another mind numbing prospect: an American Holocaust with the systematic elimination of millions of unborn babies! This is not taking place in concentration camps like Auschwitz or Dachau. It is taking place in the comfortable confines of the government-supported abortion mills like Planned Parenthood.

Since the Supreme Court decision in 1973, (Roe v. Wade), the floodgates of horrific proportions have spilled out on our nation. The essence of the decision is that: "Constitutional rights apply only after birth; hence abortion does not breach a person's right to life. States cannot regulate first trimester abortions; states can regulate but not ban second trimester abortions; and states can ban third trimester abortions."[4]

In today's society, if you want to start an all-out war of words, sometimes more than words, just mention the subject of abortion. More often than not the conversation can become red hot.

I pose one simple question: If it's wrong to stop a beating heart outside the womb, then why is it not wrong to stop a beating heart inside the womb?

Merriam-Webster.com gives a plain and simple definition to the word "abortion." It says: Abortion: a noun: abortion; plural noun: abortions: "the deliberate termination of a human pregnancy, most often performed during the first 28 weeks of pregnancy."

The Greatest Destroyer of Peace Today

On February 3, 1994, Mother Teresa spoke at the National Prayer Breakfast in Washington, DC. This woman of peace spoke boldly and without fear before an audience made of Washington elite, pastors and ministers of all faiths. The audience also included President Bill Clinton. Those in attendance soon learned never to judge a book by its cover!

Halfway through her speech, she began to talk about "the greatest destroyer of peace today." What would that be? War? Famine? Income inequality? The Billionaire Class? NO… it was abortion!

She said, "But I feel that the greatest destroyer of peace today is abortion, because it is a war against the child, a direct killing of the innocent child, murder by the mother herself.

And if we accept that a mother can kill even her own child, how can we tell other people not to kill one another? How do we persuade a woman not to have an abortion? As always, we must persuade her with love and we remind ourselves that love means to be willing to give until it hurts. Jesus gave even His life to love us. So, the mother who is thinking of abortion, should be helped to love, that is, to give until it hurts her plans, or her free time, to respect the life of her child. The father of that child, whoever he is, must also give until it hurts. By abortion, the mother does not learn to love, but kills even her own child to solve her problems.

And, by abortion, the father is told that he does not have to take any responsibility at all for the child he has brought into the world.

That father is likely to put other women into the same trouble. So abortion just leads to more abortion.

Any country that accepts abortion is not teaching its people to love, but to use any violence to get what they want. This is why the greatest destroyer of love and peace is abortion."[5]

Just the Facts

According to Abortion Statistics - United States Data & Trends the total number of abortions since the consequences of Roe V. Wade is 58,586,256.[6]

- CDC showed that 3,932,181 babies were born in the U.S. in 2013.
- In the United States, about half of all pregnancies are unintended.
- Of all unintended pregnancies, 4 in 10 are aborted.
- 21% of all pregnancies in the U.S. end in abortion, not including natural miscarriages.
- Each year, about 1.7% of all women aged 15-44 have an abortion.
- Of the women obtaining abortions in any given year, about half of them have had at least one previous abortion.
- By age 45, one-third of American women will have had at least one abortion.
- The U.S. abortion rate in 2011 was 13.9 abortions per 1,000, down from 19.4 per 1,000 in 2008.
- Women who have never been married account for one-third of abortions in America.
- Less than 1% of all abortions take place because of rape and/or incest.
- Women give an average of 3.7 reasons why they are seeking an abortion including the following:
- 21% Inadequate finances
- 21% Not ready for responsibility

- 16% Woman's life would be changed too much
- 12% Problems with relationships, unmarried
- 11% Too young and/or immature
- 8% Children are grown; she has all she wants
- 3% Baby has possible health problems
- 1% Pregnancy caused by rape/incest
- 4% Other[7]

The World is Upside Down

Think about it for a minute: we are living in a society where young people have to get their parents permission to take an aspirin at school, or sign a medical release form to play sports, but not to get an abortion.

We are now experiencing the world turned upside down. Isaiah the prophet issued a warning when he said: *"Woe to those who call evil good, and good evil; Who put darkness for light, and light for darkness; Who put bitter for sweet, and sweet for bitter! (Isaiah 5:20).*

Our upside down thinking has led us to believe that abortion providers are simply expressing compassion for those who choose not to give life to the unborn. They give the impression their only concern is for the well-being of the expectant mother. They want us to believe that the majority of abortions are provided only when it is absolutely necessary. Of course the biggest argument is that the life of the mother is threatened, or it is because of rape/incest. If anyone dare state an opposing view, they are immediately branded a bigot, racist or a woman hater.

The truth of the matter is that statistics point out only less than 1% of unwanted pregnancy is due to rape/incest. And, another little known fact is that less than 1% of all abortions are performed to save the life of the mother.

"It is morally abhorrent to use the rare cases when abortion is necessary to save the life of the mother as justification for the millions of on demand "convenience" abortions. While he was United

States Surgeon General, Dr. C. Everett Koop stated publicly that in his 38 years as a pediatric surgeon, he was never aware of a single situation in which a freeborn child's life had to be taken in order to save the life of the mother. He said the use of this argument to justify abortion in general was a "smoke screen."[8]

It is a fact that, due to medical advances, the risk and danger to a pregnant woman has declined in recent years. As far back as 1967, Dr. Alan Guttmacher of Planned Parenthood made the following statement, "Today it is possible for almost any patient to be brought through pregnancy alive, unless she suffers from a fatal illness such as cancer or leukemia, and, if so, abortion would be unlikely to prolong, much less save, life."[9]

I could list numerous examples of just how twisted the worldview has become on the issue of abortion. But, I will point out two in particular that happened during a recent football game.

CBS, which aired the game estimated that approximately 119 million people were watching. Part of the appeal of the game is to see the innovative commercials aired. I can only imagine the horror of the progressive, pro-abortion crowd when the commercial that showed a baby in an ultrasound procedure aired. The commercial considered by many as humorous and fun sent the abortion industry over the edge. Why? In the ad we see a fictitious baby kicking around in the womb as the expectant father munched on a chip.

It seems only the lobbyist for the abortion industry, the National Abortion Rights Action League (NARAL), was upset about the showing of a baby in the womb. They immediately took to Twitter in outrage, fuming, "#NotBuyingIt - that @Doritos ad using #antichoice tactic of humanizing fetuses...& sexist tropes of dads as clueless & moms as uptight. #SB50."

"If NARAL is scandalized by the notion that a human fetus is human, then they are scandalized by science," Ashley McGuire, a senior fellow with The Catholic Association, said in a statement to FoxNews.com, "We know children in the womb have distinct and human DNA. We also know that they exhibit all sorts of human behaviors in the womb such as yawning, thumb-sucking, and even dancing thanks to tremendous advances in ultrasound technology.

But groups like NARAL and Planned Parenthood rely on a denial of these scientific realities better suited to the Dark Ages to maintain their rabid insistence that those unborn babies are undeserving of basic human rights."[10]

Yet this wasn't the only commercial that was alarming to the abortion crowd. The NFL released a series of ads during the big game on the premise that statistics suggest nine months after a victory, the winning cities see a rise in births. They are commonly referred to as Super Bowl Babies.

Again, reacting to the idea of babies actually being born, NARAL tweeted, "Super Bowl Babies? Use protection, sports fans."

For the majority of us, these commercials were humorous. But, the abortion industry found nothing funny about it. You see, these commercials simply promoted the idea that life should be celebrated, not tolerated, and that life is something precious to behold. It seems that idea can be a frightening prospect for the abortion industry!

Follow the Money

Here's the ugly truth about abortion that no one wants to talk about. IT'S BIG BUSINESS! There may be no issue more hotly debated than the murder of unborn babies. But, until you see the underbelly of the abortion industry, you will not understand why there is such vehement protest against anyone who dares to speak out about the killing of the unborn. The truth is, abortion providers have a huge financial stake in the abortion industry. It appears that they will go to extraordinary lengths to stop any legislation that would end abortion.

The number one provider of abortions in the United States is Planned Parenthood. Have you ever heard anyone say that Planned

Parenthood is a private 501(c) 3 organization that simply provides health services to women? Have you ever heard a member of Congress on either side of the aisle declare that federal dollars are never used to provide abortion services? Well, I have. It's a half truth, which makes a whole LIE!

A March 3, 2015 report from LifeNews.com titled, "Why Does Planned Parenthood Get $3.6 Billion in Tax Dollars When it Makes $700 Million From Abortions?" asks and answers their own question.

The report explains, "As debate heats up in Washington over the federal budget, new research shines light on the growth in taxpayers' funding for Planned Parenthood — the largest provider of abortions in America while, according to new data, "pregnancy related services" are an ever-shrinking portion of its business.

The new report "Abortion, Inc." from Americans United for Life (AUL) provides detailed annual figures on federal funds received — making note of Planned Parenthood's overall $700 million profit in recent years, a significant sum for a 501(c)(3) non-profit charitable organization. AUL President, Dr. Charmaine Yoest, brings attention to the fact of Planned Parenthood's increased taxpayer funding since 2007, despite an economic climate where families and businesses across America have had to cut back on spending.

"Under Cecile Richards' tenure at Planned Parenthood, the number of abortions performed by Planned Parenthood has gone up," Yoest notes. "Other services like breast screenings have gone down."

In a recent interview with Bound4LIFE, Dr. Michael New of Charlotte Lozier Institute backs up these statistics. "Most of Planned Parenthood's revenue comes through performing abortions. Most people outside the pro-life movement don't know that, because public campaigns by Planned Parenthood make disingenuous claims."

To quote the AUL report: "Planned Parenthood's abortion numbers remain consistently high despite the fact that its reported overall patients substantially decreased."[11]

The bottom line is abundantly clear. Planned Parenthood does receive federal dollars, and you need to know It!

I find it interesting that abortion rights advocates will argue that every US federal budget since 1977 - including the current budget - has incorporated the Hyde amendment,[12] which directly bans federal dollars used in funding of abortion.

Like all good politicians they find a way to skirt the law to benefit those they want to benefit, and in this case it is Planned Parenthood. Under the guise of a court order, 17 states fund abortion through Medicaid. Even though, according to the most recent polls, the majority of Americans agree the federal government should not be involved in funding abortions directly – yet they continue.

In early January of 2016, Congress took steps to provide a permanent prohibition of taxpayer funding for abortion. Legislation to defund Planned Parenthood and repeal the Obamacare program that subsidizes around 1,000 health care plans that cover the costs of elective abortions. It passed in the House and is sitting in the Senate for approval.

Unfortunately, President Obama vetoed the bill. Why would he do that? According to Obama, if his own daughters made a mistake by getting pregnant, and I quote: "I don't want them punished with a baby."[13] He views these innocent babies as a punishment - not a gift.

Kill the Messenger

David Daleiden and Sandra Merritt of the Center for Medical Progress recently released a series of disturbing videos exposing the fact that Planned Parenthood harvests and sells body parts from aborted babies. The videos show that abortion procedures were changed to obtain the most "intact" specimens possible.

One would think the release of the videos exposing the corruption and criminality at Planned Parenthood would be sufficient to alert the public that such activity would not be tolerated. Surely the authorities would step up and take action. After all, it should be noted that trafficking in human body parts is also a federal felony punishable by up to 10 years in prison and a fine of $500,000.

After the release of the videos, a firestorm erupted. Planned Parenthood went on the offensive with a well-coordinated smear campaign, along with several law suits. Finally, a grand jury in Harris County, Texas, handed down an indictment.

CNN reported the following:

Washington (CNN) A Texas investigation into Planned Parenthood on Monday culminated in an indictment -- of the organization's accusers instead of the group.

The Harris County District Attorney's office announced that Planned Parenthood Gulf Coast had been cleared in the two-month-long investigation.

But the grand jury did indict two individuals who were involved in making secret recordings of the group that were released to publicly discredit the group, which provides health services and abortions.

David Daleiden and Sandra Merritt were indicted for tampering with a governmental record, a second-degree felony, and Daleiden was also indicted on the count of prohibition of the purchase and sale of human organs, a class A misdemeanor, according to the Harris County district attorney.

Texas Gov. Greg Abbott said state officials were continuing to investigate the Texas Planned Parenthood, however. "The fact remains that the videos exposed the horrific nature of abortion and the shameful disregard for human life of the abortion industry," Texas Attorney General Ken Paxton said.

Rep. Diane Black, R-Tennessee, who has led the charge against Planned Parenthood in Congress, called the decision “senseless."

"It is a sad day in America when those who harvest the body parts of aborted babies escape consequences for their actions, while the courageous truth-tellers who expose their misdeeds are handed down a politically motivated indictment instead," Black said.[14]

Spirit of Death - Cain

There is a growing trend in the area of abortion that is beginning to reveal itself in shocking ways. While the world celebrates the right to practice abortion, it does not negate the fact that taking of innocent life is strictly forbidden by God. In my book Everyone's Guide to Demons & Spiritual Warfare, I reveal the spirit of Cain. Cain is remembered for killing his innocent brother. This spirit is most often found within the family unit. Taking a baby's life with the consent of its mother while yet in the womb amounts to the most hideous and destructive thing that has ever been done to any of God's creations.

God has issued warnings in His Word about the "shedding of innocent blood" (Exodus 23:7; Deuteronomy 21:9; Isaiah 59:3-7; Proverbs 6:16-17).

In our generation, unborn babies numbering five times the entire Earth's population in the day of Christ and ten times the casualty count of World War II, have been aborted with only sporadic outcry. While certain denominations recognize "Sanctity of Life Sunday," and other para-church organizations have taken up the cause, the sad truth is the American public has been anesthetized to the holocaust that's going on right under their noses.

The spirit of Cain is not just at work in the family, but also in religious institutions, and our own hallowed halls of power. These institutions should be protecting its youngest and most vulnerable citizens. Instead they have engaged in an all-out war on them.

The spirit of Cain has wormed its way into:

• The Supreme Court who has engaged in legislating and instigating revisionist policies.

• The political system, which includes politicians in both parties and the pro-death lobbying process.
• The medical profession, including those who are performing abortions and doctors who have refused to oppose the practice.
• The legal process, including law enforcement and the court system condoning abortion and seeking to prosecute those who seek to engage in pro-life efforts.
• The educational system that has engaged in tax-funded sexual education in public schools sponsored by Planned Parenthood, secret abortions for minors, and free condoms to middle schoolers, all in the name education.
• The media, which has been used to soften the public with glorification of promiscuity and promotion of a pro-death agenda. For example: in the season-ending episode of the popular ABC show " Scandal," the female lead underwent an abortion while Silent Night was playing in the background – shame on ABC!

America is headed toward a conclusion that no one wants to think about, much less talk about. It will not stop with just aborting babies in the womb. If unabated, the death industry will continue to its natural conclusion which, according to some experts, is what they are calling after-birth abortions.

"Cain's spirit being not only alive and well, but flexing its muscles in ways that pro-abortion supporters swore would never happen" is the just published article in the Journal of Medical Ethics by professors Alberto Giubilini and Francesca Minerva.

The Journal's abstract of the article explains the professor's position clearly:

Abortion is largely accepted even for reasons that do not have anything to do with the fetus' health. By showing that (1) both fetuses and newborns do not have the same moral status as actual persons, (2) the fact that both are potential persons is morally irrelevant and (3) adoption is not always in the best interest of actual people, the authors argue that what we call 'after-birth abortion' (killing a newborn) should be permissible in all the cases where abortion is, including cases where the newborn is not disabled. This is infanticide, pure and simple, and is appearing in a peer-reviewed medical journal.

The authors conclude their article with this eye-opening statement: 'However, if a disease has not been detected during the pregnancy, if something went wrong during the delivery, or if economical, social or psychological circumstances change such that taking care of the offspring becomes an unbearable burden on someone, then people should be given the chance of not being forced to do something they cannot afford.'

You read that correctly. It's the authors' opinion that if a baby is an economic, social or psychological 'burden' for the parents, they should be allowed to put the baby to death."[15]

Are you shocked by that opinion? A selfish and self-centered culture that has no qualms about taking a baby's life will not stop just because more people are talking about it. If the unborn child is thought to be too much of a burden then the natural conclusion is to take its life, whether in the womb or after it is born.

All you have to do is read history and understand that the spirit of death has been operating for many centuries. Early history shows this to be the case:

- "Deformed infants shall be killed." - Cicero (106-43 B.C.)
- "We drown children who at birth are weakly and abnormal" - Seneca (A.D. 65)
- "A woman should submit to abortion so the state does not become too populous." - Plato
- "There is a limit fixed to the procreation of offspring...Abortion must be practiced." - Aristotle[16]

A Tale of Two Fathers

Do not be deceived, abortion is a spiritual war. It is not about constitutional rights, left or right wing politics, or who can make the best speech. It is a war between two fathers.

And I will put enmity
Between you and the woman,
And between your seed and her Seed;
He shall bruise your head,
And you shall bruise His heel.
Genesis 3:15

According to Scripture, when God spoke to Satan after the fall, He revealed the fact that two spiritual lineages would develop. Of course, I believe the last part of the verse reveals the very first prophecy about the coming of Christ.

Another thing this verse reveals is that there are two “seeds". The seed of the serpent represented by Cain and the seed of the woman represented by Seth. We know from history that these two family trees operated with two totally different agendas.

The spiritual father of Cain is Satan. Jesus pointed out this fact in a number of places when faced with the seed of Cain (John 8:38–44).

The apostle John also speaks to the heritage of Cain in 1 John 3:11-12, *“For this is the message that you heard from the beginning, that we should love one another, not as Cain who was of the wicked one and murdered his brother. And why did he murder him? Because his works were evil and his brother's righteous.”*

The spirit of Cain is the spirit of Satan, his spiritual father, who uses deception and lies to convince people that children are a hindrance to a successful and fulfilling life. Absorb the words of Dr. William Cates who wrote this statement in a paper for Planned Parenthood, "Abortion is treatment for unwanted pregnancy, the second sexually transmitted disease."[17]

But, God gives an opposite view when it comes to children. He declared children are a gift and considered a reward of the womb

(Psalm 127:3). God also declared that even before we were born He knew us, fashioned us and prepared us for a wonderful purpose and destiny (Job 10:8-12; Job 31:15; Isaiah 44:2; Luke 1:41).

The spirit of Cain will never be defeated as long as we stay silent. Whether choosing the next president of the United States, the next associate justice on the Supreme Court or our state, city and county elected officials, it is imperative that we participate in the process. It will take more than rhetoric to change a culture so filled with the spirit of Cain. We must unleash the power of the Gospel and confront the forces of evil. Then and only then will we see a shift in the American culture from death to life, and from darkness to light. Bible believing Christians are not at war with women, nor are we condemning anyone who has suffered an abortion. There is hope and grace for all.

CHAPTER SIX

THE BIG MYTH

(Islam is a Religion of Peace)

Jesus said to him, "I am the way, the truth, and the life. No one comes to the Father except through Me."
John 14:6

"The word 'Islam' means 'peace.' The word 'Muslim' means 'one who surrenders to God.' But the press makes us seem like haters."
Muhammad Ali[1]

"Let's be clear: Islam is not our adversary. Muslims are peaceful and tolerant people and have nothing whatsoever to do with terrorism."
Hillary Clinton, 2016 Candidate for the Democratic Nomination[2]

What is a myth?

According to the Merriam-Webster online dictionary it is: a traditional story, especially one concerning the early history of a people or explaining some natural or social phenomenon, and typically involving supernatural beings or events. A widely held but false belief or idea.[3]

Let's face it: fiction, myths and stories can be a lot more entertaining than facts and truth. History has given us plenty of mythical stories. Some are too far out to be believed, while others are simply lies wrapped around just enough truth to be believable. Either way, in order for a myth to exist, you have to believe everything you hear or read is true.

Taking everything at face value without investigation is generally what gives life to any myth. It's just easier to believe whatever comes your way than to discover the truth for yourself.

I intend to expose the biggest myth about Islam that has been perpetrated on the American public. It is time to look at the facts, and stop listening to the rhetoric. Just relying on the mainstream media to tell you the truth about Islam is like believing the IRS has your best financial interest at heart. It just isn't so!

Islam has declared itself to be a very violent and fascist religion, built on hate for Christians and Jews. In my opinion, it is hard to imagine a cult more evil and more duplicitous than the Islamic religion. The irony is that their plan to conquer the world is continually broadcast throughout the world on television, radio and the Internet, yet no one seems to mind except Christians. Each time we speak up, we are branded as being infected with Islamophobia.

If we don't get the sleep out of our eyes, we will wake up one day and the flag of Islam will indeed be flying over the White House. It was John F. Kennedy who said, "The great enemy of the truth is very often not the lie — deliberate, contrived and dishonest — but the myth — persistent, persuasive, and unrealistic."[4]

Myth . . . Islam is a religion of peace.

Before I give you the facts that are indisputable, I want to make it perfectly clear that I don't believe all Muslims in the United States and around the world are terrorists. I do not believe the majority have the express goal of wrapping explosives around their bodies and blowing up churches and synagogues. You have to keep in mind the enemy we face is not flesh and blood, but a demonic system of belief that has ensnared and enslaved millions of people.[5]

What is the Truth behind the myth?

America's dealings with Muslim terrorists did not begin in the twentieth century. It didn't just start with the bombing of the battleship Cole, the bombings of the World Trade Center, or countless other recent acts of terrorism.

The seeds of Muslim terrorism toward the West, and the United States in particular, go all the way back to 1786. In that year, John Adams and Thomas Jefferson met with Arab diplomats from Tunisia. Terror raids and piracy were being conducted against

American ships. These pirates became known as the "Barbary Pirates."

Thomas Jefferson wrote a letter to John Jay explaining what he believed was the primary reason for these attacks. Jefferson knew the Americans had done them no harm and tried to understand the purpose of such behavior.

Jefferson said in his letter, "We took the liberty to make some inquiries concerning the grounds of their pretensions to make war upon nations who had done them no injury, and observed that we considered all mankind as our friends who had done us no wrong, nor had given us any provocation.

The Ambassador answered us that it was founded on the Laws of their prophet, that it was written in their Koran, that all nations who should not have acknowledged their authority were sinners, that it was their right and duty to make war upon them wherever they could be found, and to make slaves of all they could take as prisoners, and that every musselman (Muslim) who should be slain in battle was sure to go to Paradise."[6]

Since 2001, two sitting Presidents have visited mosques. Both visits were intended to convey a specific message to the Muslim community.

On September 17, 2001, George W. Bush visited the Islamic Center of Washington, D.C. His visit came just sixteen days after the terrorist attack on the World Trade Center and Pentagon.

In his address, he made his purpose very clear:

"These acts of violence against innocents violate the fundamental tenets of the Islamic faith. And it's important for my fellow Americans to understand that. The English translation is not as eloquent as the original Arabic, but let me quote from the Koran, itself, 'In the long run, evil in the extreme will be the end of those who do evil. For that they rejected the signs of Allah and held them up to ridicule.' The face of terror is not the true faith of Islam. That's not what Islam is all about. Islam is peace. These terrorists don't represent peace. They represent evil and war."[7]

Fifteen years later, President Barak Obama visited a mosque located in Baltimore, Maryland. His visit occurred on February 3, 2016. Although this was not his first visit to a mosque (he visited a mosque in Cairo, Egypt after his election in 2008), it was his first visit in the United States. Obama's visit to the mosque in Baltimore became controversial because this mosque was known for its radical teachings. In 2012, it was under FBI scrutiny because its former imam condoned suicide bombing and one of its members was arrested for plotting to bomb a federal building. It is curious why he chose this particular mosque.

He, like President Bush fifteen years earlier, made his purpose clear.

He was seeking to rebut "inexcusable political rhetoric against Muslim-Americans" from Republican presidential candidates. Attempting to recast what he said was a warped image of Islam, while encouraging members of the faith to speak out against terror, Obama described Muslims as essential to the fabric of America.

"Let me say as clearly as I can as President of the United States: you fit right here," Obama told the audience at the Islamic Society of Baltimore, a 47-year-old mosque with thousands of attendees. "You're right where you belong. You're part of America, too. You're not Muslim or American. You're Muslim and American."

He continued to say that attacks on Muslims tear "at the very fabric of our nation," describing Islam as having a "tradition of peace, charity and justice . . . So let's start with this fact: For more than a thousand years, people have been drawn to Islam's message of peace. And the very word itself, Islam, comes from salam -- peace."[8]

Is Obama correct when he said "Islam" comes from "salam" which means peace? Even Muslim scholars acknowledge that "Islam" means "submission" (to Allah), that it comes from the Arabic root "aslama" meaning submission, and that "Islam" is in the command form of that verb. That's why "Muslim" means "One who submits," not "One who is peaceful."

Soon after the horrible attacks on the French satirical weekly magazine, Charlie Hebdo, which killed twelve journalists and a Paris policeman, Islamic preacher Anjem Choudary (who is co-founder of the terrorist group Al-Muhajiroun) agreed with the assessment that the word Islam does not equate to peace but submission:

He wrote: "Contrary to popular misconception, Islam does not mean peace but rather means submission to the commands of Allah alone. Therefore, Muslims do not believe in the concept of freedom of expression, as their speech and actions are determined by divine revelation and not based on people's desires."[9]

So now are we to believe that we have nothing to fear from Muslims, and they only want peace for all men? Are we to swallow the rhetoric that Islam's core belief is a tolerance toward women, homosexuals, Christians, Jews, and all others who do not share their religious beliefs?

Or, is there another agenda at work here? Is the mainstream media also complicit in its denial of radical Islamic terrorism? I could cite example after example of attacks taking place in our country, where the media seem downright recalcitrant to acknowledge even the names of the attackers.

Why do you suppose this is true? I suggest one of the main reasons is it does not fit the narrative proposed by those in positions of power. Our politically correct society does not allow criticism or blame be levied toward Muslims. It only gives a pass to those who seek to denigrate Christian/Jews.

I need to go no farther than the backyard of our church here in Chattanooga, Tennessee. On a beautiful July morning in 2015, a young man by the name of Muhammad Youssef Abdulazeez murdered four United States Marines in broad daylight. The top investigators in our nation and the news media appeared to be puzzled as to what could have prompted this young man to commit such a horrible act of violence.

From the authorities as details of the crisis unfolded:

• President Obama said it was a "lone gunman."

• White House spokesman Josh Earnest said the FBI was "looking at a variety of possible motives."

• U.S. Attorney Bill Killian said "it's premature to speculate on the motives of the shooter."

• FBI Special Agent-in-Charge Edward Reinhold said he had "no idea" what the shooter's motive was because "there is nothing that ties him to an international terror organization."

From the news media:

• Shepard Smith: "Now the search for motive."

• Don Lemon: "... too soon to know the motive."

• Lester Holt: "The motive for the attacks unknown."

• John Berman: "Any sign of a motive?"

• Paul Cruickshank: "We do not yet know the motive at this point."

• Erin Burnett: "They're desperately trying to figure out what the motive might have been."

• Wolf Blitzer: "This individual, we don't yet know the motive, Muhammad Youssef Abdulazeez."

• Joie Chen: "Investigators are already looking into the suspected shooter's background to identify some motive. The trail so far has not revealed much."

The former FBI assistant director Tom Fuentes wasn't even sure if a man named after the founder of Islam was a Muslim. Fuentes had said on CNN, "I know that what the name sounds like, but we don't know that it's a Muslim name. We know it's an Arabic name. We don't know what this individual was believing in, and that's what they're gonna be trying to determine."[10]

Is this objectivity in news coverage or fear of being politically incorrect? Do you see a pattern here? It would be logical to think after all previous terror attacks committed by Muslims, the authorities and the news media would see the pattern for themselves. Are they more afraid of being called bigots and racist than they are about finding the truth?

I wonder if the narrative we are seeing played out every day is a part of what Obama said five days before the 2008 election. "We are five days away from fundamentally transforming the United States of America."[11]

Writing an opinion piece in the Denver Post, Mike Rosen stated:

"From his first days as president, Barack Obama has stubbornly stuck to his oft-repeated mantra that 'Islam is a religion of peace.'

With the cancer of Islamist terrorism metastasizing worldwide, how much more torture, beheadings, bombings and mass murdering of "infidels" will Obama have to observe before ditching his preposterous premise? None of this carnage is committed by Hare Krishnas, Buddhists, pacifist Quakers or Mary-knoll nuns. No, it's all in the name of Allah and Islam, with a promised reward to suicide bombers of wall-to-wall virgins in an eternal orgiastic paradise. This is his religion of peace?

The kernel of truth in Obama's claim is that Islam is a religion of peace among peaceful Muslims. While Obama conveniently cherry picks peaceful clauses of the Koran, the barbaric sub-cult of Islam has plenty of Koranic ammunition to justify its holocaust supported by interpretations from prominent Islamist clerics.

Obama's refusal to acknowledge the undeniable reality of the Islamist threat imperils America and the world. In an absurd attempt at moral equivalence during his "high horse" speech at the National Prayer Breakfast, Obama scolded Christianity for its excesses in the middle ages, equating that with Islamist butchery today in the 21st century."[12]

Franklin Graham makes no apology when it comes to his views on Islam. Graham, the son of world-renowned evangelist Billy Graham, did not hold back one day after the Islamic State massacred hundreds of people in Paris, France.

"I've said this before, and many people criticized me for saying it," said Franklin Graham. "We must reform our immigration policies in the United States. We cannot allow Muslim immigrants to come across our borders unchecked while we are fighting this war on terror."

"If we continue to allow Muslim immigration, we'll see much more of what happened in Paris—it's on our doorstep," he said. "France and Europe are being overrun by young Muslim men from the Middle East, and they do not know their backgrounds or their motives and intentions."

"Islam is not a peaceful religion as George W. Bush told us and as President Barack Obama has said—that is just not true," said Rev. Graham. "Our president and our politicians in Washington need to wake up before it's too late."

"This is not the time to be politically correct," he continued. "Our nation's security is at stake. The future of our children and grandchildren is at stake."[13]

If you tell a myth (or lie) long enough, you will get people to buy into it. Unfortunately our political leaders and those who seek to defend Islam against what they consider unwarranted attacks on their religion often quote the pinnacle of Islamic beliefs found in the Quran.

I prefer to let Islam speak for itself. I offer one example where taking things out of context changes the entire meaning.

In 2009 President Obama said the following in a speech given in Cairo, Egypt:

"The Holy Quran teaches that whoever kills an innocent, it is as if he has killed all mankind; and whoever saves a person, it is as if he has saved all mankind. (Sura 5:32).

The enduring faith of over a billion people is so much bigger than the narrow hatred of a few. Islam is not part of the problem in combating violent extremism – it is an important part of promoting peace."[14]

Sounds good doesn't it? If that were the sum total of the issue, then I would agree with President Obama that the Quran does teach that Islam is a religion of peace. Unfortunately that is not the case. President Obama is misquoting the verse by taking it out of context. He is not the first, and he won't be the last to try to prop up Islam to make it something it is not.

Here is the actual translation in its context:

> *"For that cause We decreed for the Children of Israel that whosoever killeth a human being for other than manslaughter or corruption in the earth, it shall be as if he had killed all mankind, and whoso saveth the life of one, it shall be as if he had saved the life of all mankind. Our messengers came unto them of old with clear proofs (of Allah's sovereignty), but afterwards lo! Many of them become prodigals of the earth.*
>
> *The only reward for those who make war upon Allah and His messenger and strive after corruption in the land will be that they will be killed or crucified, or have their hands and feet on alternate sides cut off, or will be expelled out of the land. Such will be their degradation in the world, and in the Hereafter theirs will be an awful doom…"*
> Sura 5:32-33[15]

Do you see the significant change in tone between what Obama quoted and the context in which it was stated? Central to the understanding of the verse's meaning is what the Quran is saying when it talks about "make war" or "corruption in the earth?"

According to the writings of medieval Islamic scholar Ibn Kathir: "Wage war mentioned here means, 'oppose and contradict, and includes disbelief, blocking roads and spreading fear in the fairways. 'Corruption in the earth' or 'mischief in the land' refers to various types of evil."[16]

What he is saying is that the Quran states those who do not adhere to the teachings of Islam are waging war against the religion itself. The teachings of the Quran state that even disbelief alone is enough to justify murder and crucifixion.

The Quran also clearly says that those who do not submit to Islam are at war with Allah himself. If you are still not convinced let me quote again from the Quran:

> *"Fight those who do not believe in Allah or in the Last Day and who do not consider unlawful what Allah and His Messenger have made unlawful and who do not adopt the religion of truth from those who were given the Scripture - [fight] until they give the jizyah willingly while they are humbled."*
> Sura 9:29[17]

Do you see the implications of what Islam is teaching? If you do not submit, you are at war with Allah and all true believers. And, those who are followers of Islam are clearly instructed to go to war with you until you submit.

The Quran even allows (commands) Muslims to fight unbelievers until they gain universal Islamic worship.

> *"Say to those who have disbelieved [that] if they cease, what has previously occurred will be forgiven for them. But if they return [to hostility] - then the precedent of the former [rebellious] peoples has already taken place.*
> *And fight them until there is no fitnah and [until] the religion, all of it, is for Allah. And if they cease - then indeed, Allah is Seeing of what they do."*
> Quran 8:38-39[18]

The Hadith, (collection of reports claiming to quote the prophet Muhammad) gives permission (even commands) Muslims to fight the unbelievers:

"It is reported on the authority of Abu Huraira that the Messenger of Allah said: I have been commanded to fight against people so long as they do not declare that there is no god but Allah, and he who professed it was guaranteed the protection of his property and life on my behalf except for the right affairs rest with Allah."
Sahih Muslim 1:30[19]

Ayaan Hirsi Ali is a Dutch-American activist, author, and former politician of Somali. Her latest book was released in 2015 and is called: Heretic: Why Islam Needs a Reformation Now.

An excerpt from her book states: "For more than thirteen years now, I have been making a simple argument in response to such acts of terrorism. My argument is that it is foolish to insist, as our leaders habitually do, that the violent acts of radical Islamists can be divorced from the religious ideals that inspire them. Instead we must acknowledge that they are driven by a political ideology, an ideology embedded in Islam itself, in the holy book of the Qur'an as well as the life and teachings of the Prophet Muhammad contained in the hadith.

Let me make my point in the simplest possible terms: Islam is not a religion of peace. For expressing the idea that Islamic violence is rooted not in social, economic, or political conditions—or even in theological error—but rather in the foundational texts of Islam itself, I have been denounced as a bigot and an "Islamophobe." I have been silenced, shunned, and shamed. In effect, I have been deemed to be a heretic, not just by Muslims—for whom I am already an apostate—but by some Western liberals as well, whose multicultural sensibilities are offended by such "insensitive" pronouncements."[20]

Another part of the ongoing narrative concerning Islam is that Muslims, Christians and Jews worship the same God. If that is true, I suggest we rethink the whole issue. It is not true, in spite of the progressive agenda that continues to perpetuate the myth that Islam is on the same level as Judeo-Christian faith in every way. While it's true there are certain similarities due to the fact that Mohammed plagiarized much of the Christian Bible and Torah as it relates to Judaism and Christianity, let it be known that is as far as it goes.

This mythology was highlighted recently by House Minority Leader Nancy Pelosi (D-CA) who spoke at the National Prayer Breakfast in Washington DC. She did her best to present an argument that Christianity, Judaism and Islam are at their heart – the same.

She said: "As we hear these words from John 13:15 and 17, we know that this message, this command of love, is not confined to New Testament. The same message stands at the center of the Torah and the teachings of the Prophet Mohammad too.

From the Torah it says, 'Love your neighbor as yourself.' And from Muhammad, 'None of you has faith until he loves for his brother or his neighbor what he loves for himself."[21]

Here's what John 13:15-17 says: *"For I have given you an example, that you should do as I have done to you. Most assuredly, I say to you, a servant is not greater than his master; nor is he who is sent greater than he who sent him. If you know these things, blessed are you if you do them."*

Is it true that Mohammed and Jesus are on equal footing? Is it true that Christians and Muslims worship the same God? Is it true that each, at its core, is a religion of peace and security?
Below are a few examples…you decide for yourself:

• Muhammad…"Allah does not love those who reject Islam." (Quran 30:45, 3:32, 22:38)

• Jesus said, God loves everyone (John 3:16).

• Muhammad…"I have been commanded to fight against people till they testify that there is no god but Allah, and that Muhammad is the messenger of Allah" (Muslim 1:33)

• Jesus said, "He who lives by the sword will die by the sword." (Matthew 26:52)

• Muhammad..."Stoned women for adultery." (Muslim 4206)

• Jesus said, "Let he who is without sin cast the first stone." (John 8:7)

• Muhammad..."Owned and traded slaves." (Sahih Muslim 3901)

• Jesus neither owned nor traded slaves.

• Muhammad..."Beheaded 800 Jewish men and boys." (Abu Dawud 4390)

• Jesus beheaded no one.

• Muhammad..."Jihad in the way of Allah elevates one's position in Paradise by a hundred fold." (Muslim 4645)

• Jesus said, "Blessed are the peacemakers, for they will be called Sons of God." (Matthew 5:9)

• Muhammad..."Married 13 wives and kept sex slaves." (Bukhari 5:268, Quran 33:50)

• Jesus was celibate.

• Muhammad...Slept with a 9-year-old child. (Sahih Muslim 3309, Bukhari 58:236)

• Jesus did not have sex with children.[22]

I must relate one more example of the global attempt to meld Islam, Judaism and Christianity into a singular faith. This is not coming from the news media, or political leaders. No, this is from a member of the so-called "Christian community" who is espousing some of the most ridiculous propositions I have ever heard.

From Baptist Pastor Steve Chalke:

"There are Christians who worship a militant, violent God," said Steve Chalke, pastor and founder of the UK-based Oasis charity. "There are Christians who worship a God who doesn't want women in leadership. There are Christians who worship a God who says if you are gay you will burn in hell. There are Christians who worship a God who does not believe in global warming." Chalke said that these aberrant forms of Christianity are further from the gospel of Jesus than many Muslim beliefs.

"I know some emphases in Islamic teaching come closer to the teaching of Christ and the Bible than some teaching in Western churches," he said.

Chalke also affirmed his belief that all believers ultimately worship one and the same God, even if they understand him in different ways.

"As individuals we all worship different shades of the same God," he said. "If we say Islam is an evil religion and they worship a different God and Christianity is the only way to heaven then we are heading for World War Three," he added.[23]

If we are not careful we will fall prey to the enemy's lies and become discouraged. Although it will never be reported in the mainstream media, I am receiving reports from various sources that the fires of revival are breaking out in the Muslim community. According to a recent report broadcast on CBN, many Muslims from every corner of the world are responding to the good news of the gospel.

"I see many, many Arabic-speaking people turning to Christ, accepting Him as Lord and Savior," said Nizar Shaheen, host of Light for the Nations, a Christian program seen throughout the Muslim world. "It's happening all over the Arab world. It's happening in North Africa. It's happening in the Middle East. It's happening in the Gulf countries. It's happening in Europe and Canada and the United States-in the Arabic-speaking world. Everywhere, people are accepting Jesus."

"What's happening nowadays in the Muslim world has never happened before," said Father Zakaria Boutros, an Egyptian Coptic priest who is one of the foremost evangelists to the Muslim world. He says a cross-section of Muslims are accepting Jesus Christ. "Young and old, educated and not educated, males and females, even those who are fanatic."

Heidi Baker, PhD, a Christian Missionary and the President and CEO of Iris Global, sees thousands of African Muslims receiving Jesus and getting baptized. "It's probably the only place in the world where they are coming so quickly," she said. "Many people are having dreams. They see Jesus appear to them. Probably half our pastors were leaders, imams in Moslem mosques. They were leaders in these mosques, now they're pastors."[24]

DON'T GIVE UP...THERE IS HOPE!

CHAPTER SEVEN

THE GRAND ILLUSION

(The "Hoax" of Borrowing Your Way to Wealth)

He who loves silver will not be satisfied with silver;
nor he who loves abundance, with increase.
This also is vanity.
Ecclesiastes 5:10

"I contend that for a nation to try to tax itself into prosperity is like a man standing in a bucket and trying to lift himself up by the handle."
Winston S. Churchill[1]

History is full of scams, frauds, and financial hoaxes that removed billions of dollars from the pockets of investors and destroyed entire economies, but none of them compare to the damage caused by Bernie Madoff's Ponzi scheme involving over $18 billion. The fact that Madoff was able to keep the scheme going for so long is ample testament to the fact that the U.S. government -- despite repeated scandals, frauds, rip-off, hoaxes, and general fancy mischief -- isn't really serious about regulating the financial sector. The SEC even investigated his operations and failed to find anything wrong, even though the impossibility of his business model was staring them in the face.[2]

While we deplore the actions of those who would rip off and otherwise steal money from innocent people, we seem to have more tolerance for government officials who tell lies, shift numbers and create the grand illusion of financial stability.

For most of us, talk about interest rates, inflation statistics and monetary policy is outside of our expertise. Just try to carry on a conversation about job market participation and inflation data with the average person, then watch their eyes roll back in their head. That attitude is just fine with the federal government. These overpaid fat-cats are more than happy for the American people to live in a fantasyland with their eyes closed and leave the boring details to the experts in Washington DC. At least that is what it apppears that they hope for.

More people are starting to tune in and ask serious questions about what is going on in the nation's capital. The atmosphere is changing and the cover up is being exposed for what it is - a grand illusion!

The year was 2009. You may remember during those days that President Obama's Affordable Care Act was being pushed hard by the administration. In July of that year, Vice President Joe Biden, along with Health and Human Services Director Kathleen Sibelius, spoke at a town hall meeting hosted by AARP. Doing his best to convince those in attendance that unless the Democrat supported healthcare plan became law, the nation would go bankrupt, Biden emphasized that the only way to avoid that fate was for the government to spend more money.

"And folks look, AARP knows and the people working here today know, the president knows, and I know, that the status quo is simply not acceptable," Biden said at an event in Alexandria, Va. "It's totally unacceptable. And it's completely unsustainable. Even if we wanted to keep it the way we have it. We can't do it financially."

"We're going to go bankrupt as a nation," Biden said. "Well, people when I say that look at me and say, 'What are you talking about? You're telling me we have to go spend money to keep from going bankrupt?'" Biden said. "The answer is yes, I'm telling you."[3]

Of course we now know that most of the promises made during those early days turned out to be false. But the point is that we must look behind the façade of promises and understand the general philosophy the vice president articulated. It is certainly not a new philosophy, but to actually hear it spoken out loud is almost beyond belief. And what is the philosophy? Again, in his own words... "we have to go spend money to keep from going bankrupt?"

Can a government really borrow and spend its way to prosperity? Is it possible to spend more than you take in and not go over the economic cliff? At this writing, our nation is more than $18 trillion in debt. And, if that is not enough to keep you up at night, the government is adding approximately $4.2 billion to the debt each day.

So, who will pay for this reckless economic policy? Mike Patton wrote in Forbes magazine an analysis of what the national debt means to the individual household in America.

He stated, "In 2004, the federal debt was $7.3 trillion. This rose to $10 trillion when the housing bubble burst four years later. Today it exceeds $18 trillion and is projected to approach $21 trillion by 2019. When you break this down to an amount per taxpayer, the numbers are substantial. It has more than doubled over the past 11 years, rising from $72,051 per taxpayer in 2004 to $154,161 today. As the debt continues higher, the liability of every taxpayer is also rising. The change in the amount of the federal debt per taxpayer from 2004 to 2015 represents an average annual increase of 7.16%. This is much more than the average annual wage increase during the same period."

He went on to state that the federal government is mortgaging the future earnings of an entire generation, "Excessive debt was also one of the primary catalysts for the economic boom of the 1980s, 1990s and part of the 2000s. However, when debt is used in excess, it steals from the future since it must be repaid. This is because a dollar borrowed today necessitates that a dollar plus interest be repaid in the future. This reduces the amount of money available for future spending. If the amount of debt accumulated is significant and the period of accumulation is long, the required debt payments will negatively impact economic growth."[4]

The federal government is borrowing money on a colossal scale. Some say it is unprecedented except for World War II. The Federal Reserve is printing money and dumping cash into the banks with a monetary philosophy that is mortgaging the future of our nation. We are a debtor nation:

- We owe most of the money to ourselves.
- We owe a big chunk of the money — about $6 trillion — to the Federal government. So if there ever were a default the gov-

ernment would also be stiffing itself.

- We owe about $5 trillion to other countries, including China.
- The total debt to China is $1.3 trillion.[5]

Applying the government's principles of "spending more than you take in" to your individual household would be an unmitigated disaster. It would not take long for you to lose everything you own, or ever hope to own.

When a family has financial difficulties, it usually take steps to correct the situation, like delaying the purchase of a new car, cutting up credit cards and putting off a home renovation.

This philosophy of borrowing your way to economic health tells us to buy more, finance more and get back to spending more cash when times are tough. How long do you think a financial counselor would stay in business if he adopted that philosophy when counseling clients who are struggling financially? This economic plan is totally opposite of what the average wise citizen would do when faced with economic trouble.

Let's face it, if borrowing more money and spending more than we take in actually brought prosperity, then it would be a model for every nation in the world. Nations that employ this kind of financial lunacy eventually fall over the cliff.

The Lure of Socialism

In tough economic times people are always looking for alternatives. With lower wages, a shrinking middle class, and a general discontent with all politicians, the atmosphere is ripe for a different direction. So, along comes something old, something borrowed and something that sounds a lot like warmed over socialism.

Who wouldn't be charmed with promises of free college, free health care and higher minimum wages? Being taken care of by the government from the "cradle to the grave" is a dream world for those who think that working for something is a curse, not a blessing.

In the 2016 election cycle, we not only have candidates who are promoting socialist beliefs, but have an openly socialist candidate running for the highest office in the land. The battle cry of the modern democratic/socialist movement is - "Let's be like the Scandinavian countries!" The truth is that a certain percentage of the population is falling for the oldest scam known to man, "You can get something for nothing!"

The current "gimme" generation has a very short attention span. They have forgotten that the most demonic ideology the world has ever known was The National Socialist German Worker's Party, better known as the Nazi Party. It rose to power following Germany's defeat in World War I. The Nazis preyed upon the discontent of the people by attacking big business and capitalism and using class-warfare as a tool to further its popularity, establishing a culture of entitlement and ideological superiority. Racism was also a key element in the spread of this toxic ideology, and resulted in the murder of six million Jews during the Holocaust.

Today, we are hearing the same old tired ideas re-packaged with new phrases designed to prey on the emotions of an unsuspecting public. Have we become so short-sighted that we won't heed the hard-fought lessons we have learned from the past 80 years? Has our education system become such a cesspool of ideologues and history revisionists that our children are being brainwashed into believing that socialism is the answer to all of the problems that ail us as a nation? Oh sure... socialism has its appeal — after all, who doesn't like FREE STUFF?

The problem is that nothing is free. Even "free" stuff is costing someone, somewhere.

Take education for example. One of the mantras we are hearing is "free education/free college." If college becomes free, one would have to assume that all of those things it takes to keep the doors open — lights, heat, electricity, etc. — are all going to be free as well.

And how about the salaries of all who work at universities? If we are going to offer free college, would it not be reasonable to assume that all of the college faculties will be doing their jobs gratis? That means janitors, security, administration, and yes . . . professors. So, all of these (mostly highly) trained and educated people are going to put in their 40+ hours per week with no paycheck for their labor. Sure, there are those states where some college is being offered for "free" (Tennessee being one that offers 2 years of community college for "free"). However, "free" is still not free . . . it ultimately comes at the expense of the taxpayer.

It was former British Prime Minister Margaret Thatcher who said, "The trouble with socialism is that eventually you run out of other people's money"[6]

Early in our history, founding father Thomas Jefferson had much to say about the danger of socialism. He understood the attraction of socialism and the inclination to live well on government assistance while exerting as little work effort and initiative as possible. Jefferson knew that politicians have used the attraction of socialistic promises to gain great power.

In reflecting on the fall of Rome, he paraphrased the words of Cicero to shed light on the danger..."The budget should be balanced, the Treasury should be refilled, public debt should be reduced, the arrogance of officialdom should be tempered and controlled, and the assistance to foreign lands should be curtailed lest Rome become bankrupt. People must again learn to work, instead of living on public assistance." Cicero (paraphrased) 55 BC[7]

Jefferson also issued a warning to us and our posterity..."To take from one because it is thought that his own industry and that of his father's has acquired too much, in order to spare to others, who, or whose fathers have not exercised equal industry and skill, is to violate arbitrarily the first principle of association -- the guarantee to every one of a free exercise of his industry and the fruits acquired by it."[8]

Socialism and all related "isms" are nothing more than a "grand illusion!" It is deception at the highest level. While our country is on the fast track to economic ruin, the politicians on both sides of the spectrum play a shell game with the American public. Covering the terms "socialism" and "communism" with "liberal" and "progressive" will never hide the truth about what they are and their intended result. To create a dependent electorate which will always vote for the party that gives away the most free stuff is just what we see on the surface. The underlying issue is power! He who controls the "stuff" controls the power to dictate the everyday life of its citizens. And, anyone who dares to talk about cutting, scaling back, or eliminating some of these handouts is immediately branded a bigot.

The further we run as a society from the teachings and statutes of the Bible, the further and faster we run toward our own destruction. Although appearing to tolerate Christianity initially, the Nazis moved rapidly to quell the voice of the Christian church, while simultaneously forming an unholy alliance with Islam. Martin Bormann, Hitler's personal secretary, once admitted, "National Socialism and Christianity are irreconcilable."[9] We are seeing the dark specters of this type of ideology taking hold in our nation with Christians being put on trial for their beliefs and convictions, while Islam is given a pass and a warm embrace by those in the corridors of power. In the end, however, it's quite simple, one cannot forsake the teachings and statutes of the One who established human civilization without severe consequences.

Money, wealth and power are consistent themes from Wall Street to Main Street. Even the Church has fallen prey to this deception, and more church leaders have succumbed to the "buy now, pay later" philosophy of the Federal Government.

The Bible is not silent when it comes to money and a good work ethic. Instead of being shameful and cursed, hard work is considered admirable and Godly.

When it comes to wealth, the Scripture expresses a different point of view. While most view wealth only in terms of money, the truth is that you can amass wealth and still be poor. Throughout my ministry, I have encountered many people who had plenty of money, yet their lives were bankrupt. Money was plentiful, but it was not the answer.

The apostle Paul put wealth in its proper perspective when he said, *"And my God shall supply all of your need according to His riches in glory by Christ Jesus" (Philippians 4:13).*

His definition of wealth was, *"being provided for through an unlimited supply."* You see, wealth must be viewed in light of present need. For example, the most present need may be healing for a family member, peace of mind, a new job, or the return of a rebellious child. These things may be more pressing than a large bank account. According to the money mongers, financial wealth is the end of itself, but God's ultimate will for us is that we be made whole.

It is time to turn from the financial gurus who have put us in this mess to begin with and start reading again the best financial management book that has ever been written – The Bible.

There is a spirit at work in our nation that must be confronted. Those who have eyes to see and ears to hear will recognize it immediately. It is determined to destroy the foundation of our churches, and the underpinning of our government.

The Spirit of Poverty is at Work

Poverty is not exclusive to living in a ghetto or growing up in the most rundown part of town. Being poor does not come as the result of a higher unemployment rate or the lack of qualifying skills. These are the "fruit" of poverty, not the "root" of poverty. Being "broke" is a temporary condition that can be remedied with hard work and smart financial planning. The spirit of poverty is a destructive demonic spirit that robs people of their dreams, goals, motivations, and desires.

Have you ever heard the phrase “poverty-stricken?" This alludes to the concept that poverty is something that comes upon a person, family, church, community or nation. Why haven’t all of the social programs available to Americans eradicated poverty? Billions have been spent to eliminate hunger and poverty and yet the problem is greater today than ever before. The United States is a giving nation. We have given billions of dollars in foreign aid to poor nations in order to help them get a foothold on the economic ladder. In spite of our best efforts to throw money at problems around the world, it seems our efforts for the most part have been futile. The more money we give, the less improvement we see.

Consider Haiti 5 years after a deadly Earthquake

In the immediate aftermath of the 7.0-magnitude quake, heart-rending images from the island spurred Americans to open their wallets for victims in the poorest country in the Western hemisphere.

They gave $1.4 billion to relief and recovery efforts over the course of the next year, according to an analysis by the Chronicle of Philanthropy. Of that, $32 million alone came in the form of $10 text messages to the American Red Cross. Americans texted tens of millions of dollars in donations and governments gave billions, but five years after an earthquake left corpses and rubble piled across Haiti, 85,000 people still live in crude displacement camps and many more in deplorable conditions.

The United Nations said that in total, $13.34 billion has been earmarked for the crisis through 2020, though two years after the quake, less than half of that amount had actually been released, according to U.N. documents. The U.S. government has allocated $4 billion; $3 billion has already been spent, and the rest is dedicated to longer-term projects.

Some global development analysts say that the spending structure—with the vast majority of money being funneled through foreign contractors instead of the Haitian government or local organizations—has built-in inefficiencies, compounded by a lack of accountability and transparency.

The disconnect between the massive amount of private and public aid, and the poverty, disease and homelessness that still plague the country raises a question that critics say is too difficult to answer: Where did all that money go?[10]

On the home front, the current White House administration has been hard at work to redistribute wealth and create a socialist utopia, and yet there are more people living on food stamps and government assistance than any time in our nation's history.

Did you know that as of the last quarter of 2014, there were 46,674,364 people on food stamps in the United States? This number exceeded the populations of Columbia (46,245,297), Kenya (46,245,297), Ukraine (44,291,413) and Argentina (43,024,374).[11]

Author Bill Moyers asked..."Why are record numbers of Americans on food stamps? Because record numbers of Americans are in poverty. Why are people falling through the cracks? Because there are cracks to fall through."[12] While Moyers makes a valid point about the true condition of the problem, he, like other liberal thinkers, has only one solution – throw more money at the problem. I say again, if money alone was the answer, poverty would have been eliminated with Franklin D. Roosevelt's New Deal, and Lyndon B. Johnson's "War on Poverty."

The New Normal . . . Is Not Normal

Listening to the mainstream media telling us that, even though the economy is not what it once was, we shouldn't fear, is like going to the doctor and being told you have a terminal illness, but not to worry because you are not going to die today.

It is not normal for the federal government to keep pumping cash and credit into the economy to keep things from getting out of hand. It is not normal for the Central Bank to lend money below the rate of consumer price inflation. It is not normal for the government to spend $1.50 for every dollar it receives in tax revenue.

Here's how the deception works: If you keep doing things that aren't exactly normal long enough, people will eventually think that what you're doing is normal, and stop asking questions.

Economist Bill Bonner explains how this madness all began. "The feds didn't invent their EZ money theories. John Maynard Keynes came up with the goofy program many years ago. He met with Franklin Roosevelt and explained the idea. Roosevelt later confessed that he had no idea what Keynes was talking about. But he liked Keynes' palaver, because it gave him a theoretical justification for taking control of the economy.

Keynes' basic idea was stolen from the Old Testament. Pharaoh stored up grain during the years when harvests were good. Then, he gave out the grain when they were bad. He looked like a genius. FDR probably wanted to look like a genius too.

But governments found it a lot easier to spend during the lean years than to save during the fat ones. In practice, they didn't save at all. And then, when trouble came, they had no real resources with which to do any good.

Instead, they could only borrow money...or print it.

The real problem now is that the private sector has debt to settle. But you can't settle debt with more debt. No, dear reader, you can't borrow your way out of debt. But you can sure in-debt your way out of borrowing. That is, you can run up so much debt that no one wants to lend you any more money."[13]

The Bible is Clear

In Scripture, poverty is nearly always connected with unrighteousness. It was the "unrighteousness" of an individual or the nation as a whole that brought oppression upon the people of God.

A perfect example is found in 1Kings 17. An evil king by the name of Ahab allowed idol worship into the land. As a result of this blatant rejection of God, judgment was swift and sure, and poverty and barrenness covered the land. No nation can turn its back on God and expect to be blessed. Throughout Scripture you will see, in most cases, that God's judgment on an unrepentant nation (or individual) usually begins with the economy (Leviticus 26:14-39; Deuteronomy 28:15-68; Psalm 37:38; Isaiah 13:11; Zephaniah 1:12; 1 Thessalonians 4:6).

This spirit of poverty can become a chain so heavy that, until it is confronted, people will struggle and never know why. Instead of turning to the one book that can provide answers, they will search for alternatives and still come up empty.

Solomon identified 5 links in the chain of poverty:

1. Refusing instruction

Poverty and shame will come to him who disdains correction, but he who regards a rebuke will be honored.
Proverbs 13:18

2. Following after failures

He who tills his land will have plenty of bread, but he who follows frivolity will have poverty enough!
Proverbs 28:19

3. Withholding more than you need

There is one who scatters, yet increases more; and there is one who withholds more than is right, but it leads to poverty.
Proverbs 11:24

4. Motivated to Get Rich Quick

A faithful man will abound with blessings, but he who hastens to be rich will not go unpunished.
Proverbs 28:20

5. Laziness

He who has a slack hand becomes poor, but the hand of the diligent makes rich. He who gathers in summer is a wise son; he who sleeps in harvest is a son who causes shame.
Proverbs 10:4-5

Solomon also pointed out the joy and blessing of hard work:

1. Working hard is a matter of self-control

Whoever has no rule over his own spirit is like a city broken down, without walls.
Proverbs 25:28

2. Working hard produces great benefits

He who tills his land will be satisfied with bread, but he who follows frivolity is devoid of understanding.
Proverbs 12:11

3. Working hard reduces stress

In all labor there is profit, but idle chatter leads only to poverty. The crown of the wise is their riches, but the foolishness of fools is folly.
Proverbs 14:23-24

4. Working hard brings satisfaction

The desire of the lazy man kills him, for his hands refuse to labor. He covets greedily all day long, but the righteous gives and does not spare.
Proverbs 21:25-26

5. Working hard opens the door for new opportunities

Do you see a man who excels in his work? He will stand before kings; he will not stand before unknown men.
Proverbs 22:2

The Apostle Paul was also pretty direct on the issue of work:

Let him who stole steal no longer, but rather let him labor, working with his hands what is good, that he may have something to give him who has need.
Ephesians 4:28

And whatever you do, do it heartily, as to the Lord and not to men, knowing that from the Lord you will receive the reward of the inheritance; for you serve the Lord Christ.
Colossians 3:23-24

But if anyone does not provide for his own, and especially for those of his household, he has denied the faith and is worse than an unbeliever.
1 Timothy 5:8

For even when we were with you, we commanded you this: If anyone will not work, neither shall he eat. For we hear that there are some who walk among you in a disorderly manner, not working at all, but are busybodies. Now those who are such we command and exhort

through our Lord Jesus Christ that they work in quietness and eat their own bread.
2Thessalonians 3:10-12

Who is pulling the purse strings? It is time for America to wake up! Wake up America! You can't borrow your way to wealth, nor can you spend your way out of debt. It has never worked before and it will not work now. It was Ralph Waldo Emerson who said, "Without ambition one starts nothing. Without work one finishes nothing. The prize will not be sent to you. You have to win it."[14]

CHAPTER EIGHT

SHOWDOWN

(Exposing the Homosexual Agenda)

For this reason God gave them up to vile passions. For even their women exchanged the natural use for what is against nature. Likewise also the men, leaving the natural use of the woman, burned in their lust for one another, men with men committing what is shameful, and receiving in themselves the penalty of their error which was due.

Romans 1:26-27

"If you're involved in the gay and lesbian lifestyle, it is bondage. It is personal bondage, personal despair and personal enslavement."
Former Minnesota State Senator Michele Bachmann[1]

It has been building for some time now. A showdown of epic proportion is taking center stage and if we don't engage now, we never will. Over the last fifty years, there has been an agenda at work that you might have missed unless you were paying close attention. Now that our eyes are fully open, we can see where the battle lines are drawn.

Be honest . . . did you ever think we could, as a nation, descend so far in such a short period of time? Did you think we would go from a nation holding to strong Christian values, to what we are embracing today?

The church's involvement in the culture has been a source of conflict for as long as I can remember. There have been many controversies about the role of the church, especially when it came to acting as a moral center of the community. There was a time when the center of authority was the local church. From small towns to big cities, the local church was the final word on all matters involving morality and virtue. Sadly that day has long passed.

But no issue compares to the current cultural phenomenon as clearly as homosexuality. Like a tidal wave, the homosexual agenda has swept over the American landscape, even to the point that some major denominations are capitulating to the demands of the agenda put forth by those who want to reshape the culture.

The Design of the Homosexual Agenda

Don't think for a minute the shift of attitudes toward the homosexual lifestyle just happened by chance or occurred by a random series of coincidences. There was a strategy in place to shape and utterly transform America. You don't have to be an Ivy League scholar to see how successful it has been.

There are professionals who have dedicated their lives to influencing the culture toward products and services they represent. Most of these men and women worked behind the scenes so you probably don't know the face behind the jingle or slogan.

You may never have heard of Dan Wieden, co-founder of Wieden & Kennedy advertising agency. He and his professional team came up with a slogan in 1988 that has been repeated by millions. If you have seen a Nike commercial you know it very well... "Just do it" has been reverberating in the ears of sports fans for almost 30 years. Dan Wieden is just one of many brilliant marketing strategists who has been successfully nudging the culture toward a particular product.

Let me offer you two more names that may not be familiar to you, yet we are seeing and feeling their influence to this very hour. Marshall Kirk and Hunter Madsen are the two men most responsible for transforming the American culture's attitude toward the gay lifestyle. Their work has been strategic, slow and subtle with a definite intentionality.

In the November 1987 edition of Guide, a magazine for homosexuals, the two men authored an article titled, "The Overhauling of Straight America." It was Kirk, a researcher in neuropsychiatry, and Madsen, a public relations consultant, who laid out a blueprint to fundamentally change America's attitudes toward homosexuals and homosexuality. In 1989, they expanded that blueprint into a 398-page book titled After the Ball: How America Will Conquer Its Fear and Hatred of Gays in the 90s.[2]

What was the goal? It was a simple and straightforward strategy designed to make homosexuality "acceptable," and if anyone disagreed, they would be branded as insensitive at best, and a homophobe at worst. Their strategy was to make it so uncomfortable for anyone to disagree with the gay lifestyle that any speech directed toward homosexuality would be branded as hate speech.

They tackled the most difficult issue first which was changing the minds of the American public concerning homosexuals and homosexual rights. Little by little, they desensitized the public, changing their view from hostility and condemnation to indifference. "She likes strawberry and I like vanilla; he follows baseball and I follow football. It's no big deal."[3]

These men had no illusions as to the culture of the late 80s. They knew what they were up against and the transformation would not come overnight. Unlike many who claim to be Bible believing Christians, who stop at the first sign of opposition, these men set a course of action and would not be deterred.

They said: "At least in the beginning we are seeking public desensitization and nothing more. We do not need and cannot expect a full 'appreciation' or 'understanding' of homosexuality from the average American. You can forget about trying to persuade the masses that homosexuality is a good thing. But if you can only get them to think that is just another thing... then your battle for legal and social rights is virtually won."[4]

How successful were they? Well, consider how the views have changed on the issue of homosexuality since their article first appeared in 1987, followed by their 360 page book published in 1989.

Gallup polls showed the following:

• In 1987, only 33% agreed that same-sex relations between consenting adults should be legal.

• In 1987, 55% thought homosexuality should be outlawed. (The numbers don't add up because some people refused to give an opinion).

- By 2015, the numbers reversed. 68% believed such sexual relations should be legal and only 28% were opposed.

What about same-sex marriage? The Gallup poll did not even bother with the issue because it was not something on the mind of the general public. In 1996, when the first polls were conducted, only 27% approved while 68% were opposed. But in 2015, the polls showed that 58% approved and 40% disapproved, another startling reversal in attitudes.

In 1989, the poll showed only 19% of Americans believed people were born homosexual, with 48% believing it was due to other factors, such as upbringing and other environmental influences. Once again, in 2015, the numbers reversed with 51% believing that homosexuals were born, therefore it was in their DNA, and only 30% attributing it to other factors. This is in spite of the fact that extensive genetic research, including many studies of identical twins where only one was homosexual, have disproven genetic determinism.[5]

The spirit of antichrist works through deception. What has been perpetrated on the American culture concerning homosexuality is nothing more than what the apostle Paul warned us about in 2 Corinthians 2:11, *"Lest Satan should take advantage of us; for we are not ignorant of his devices (schemes)."*

The sad truth is that many weak and timid preachers were intimidated and bullied from speaking up and speaking out. Instead of calling sin by its name and pointing those trapped in the homosexual lifestyle to the freedom that comes from the gospel of Jesus Christ, they bowed down before the altar of political correctness. It is a proven fact that when truth is not spoken, evil will flourish.

What was their design (deception) that proved so effective? They laid out a six point blueprint for success. It was simple and straightforward – and it worked.

Step 1: Don't stop talking about it

Authors Kirk and Madsen say that, "Almost any behavior begins to look normal if you are exposed to enough of it. The way to numb raw sensitivities about homosexuality is to have a lot of people talk a great deal about the subject in a neutral or supportive way. Constant talk builds the impression that public opinion is at least divided on the subject, and that a sizable segment accepts or even practices homosexuality."

They continue to lay out their strategy, "And when we say talk about homosexuality, we mean just that. In the early stages of any campaign to reach straight America, the masses should not be shocked and repelled by premature exposure to homosexual behavior itself. Instead, the imagery of sex should be downplayed. First, let the camel get his nose inside the tent—only later his unsightly derriere!

They go on to say: "When we are exposed to anything repeatedly, it becomes routine and normal. What initially might shock someone eventually can become acceptable. And acceptability is the ultimate goal. What at one time was highly offensive to the vast majority of Americans is now no big deal. They've been lulled into complacency."[6]

Step 2: You must portray gays as victims

Kirk and Madsen wrote: "In any campaign to win over the public, gays must be cast as victims in need of protection." This does not try to deal with the issue of whether it is right or wrong to live the gay lifestyle. It is just an attempt to manipulate others with the motive of getting them to accept values they otherwise wouldn't agree with.

"If gays are presented, instead, as a strong and prideful tribe promoting a rigidly nonconformist and deviant lifestyle, they are more likely to be seen as a public menace of resistance and oppression. For that reason, we must forego the temptation to strut our 'gay pride' publicly when it conflicts with the Gay Victim image. This means that jaunty mustachioed musclemen would keep very low profile in gay commercials and other public presentations, while sympathetic figures of nice young people, old people, and attractive women would be featured."[7]

Step 3: Give protectors a just cause

Author Charles Melear continued to unmask the strategic plan of Kirk and Madsen: "A media campaign that casts gays as society's victims and encourages straights to be their protectors must make it easier for those to respond, to assert and explain their new protectiveness. Few straight women, and even fewer straight men, will want to defend homosexuality boldly as such ... Our campaign should not demand direct support for homosexual practices, [but] should instead take anti-discrimination as its theme"[8]

Step 4: Make gays look good

"In order to make a gay victim sympathetic to straights, you have to portray him as everyman. But an additional theme of the campaign should be more aggressive and upbeat: to offset the increasingly bad press that these times have brought to homosexual men and women, the campaign should paint gays as superior pillars of society."[9]

I would say this approach has been immensely successful. Another area that Kirk and Madsen pointed out is the importance of the celebrity endorsement. Whether the celebrity is straight or gay is not the salient issue, but whether they are willing to endorse the gay lifestyle as normal.

Having a celebrity stand on stage to receive an award while at the same time advocating and applauding the gay lifestyle fits right into the narrative to gain a wider acceptance to the general public.

Step 5: Make the victimizers look bad

"At a later stage of the media campaign for gay rights it will be time to get tough with remaining opponents. To be blunt, they must be vilified. Our goal here is twofold: First, we seek to replace the mainstream's self-righteous pride about its homophobia with shame and guilt. Second, we intend to make the anti-gays look so nasty that average Americans will want to dissociate themselves from such types. The public should be shown images of ranting homophobes whose secondary traits and beliefs disgust middle America."[10]

All you have to do is turn on your television to see how this part of the strategy has succeeded. Their goal was to link the anti-gay rhetoric to something like you would hear at a KKK rally, or Nazi propaganda leveled at the Jews in the 1930s. The battle cry was, "If you oppose gay rights, same-sex marriage or the gay lifestyle, you are bigoted and anti-American!"

Step 6: Solicit funds: The buck stops here

"Any massive campaign of this kind would require unprecedented expenditures for months or even years—an unprecedented fundraising drive"[11]

If you've ever wondered why so many American businesses cater to a gay clientele, donate money to support homosexual causes, and celebrated the U.S. Supreme Court's ruling legalizing same-sex marriage, it's because they understand that generally, homosexual couples, who typically don't have children, have substantially more discretionary income than families who do.

This is also being felt in the political arena, where wealthy gays help bankroll campaigns for sympathetic candidates who will advance their interests, and fund ads attacking those who stand for traditional and biblical values.[12]

The Direction of the of the Homosexual Agenda

Where is all of this headed? The free love sexual revolution of the 60's that many Americans looked on as a fad and something to be chided, has now morphed into a sexual freedom that most people never anticipated. Morality has been redefined, which is something our founding fathers likely never foresaw. We are now living in a nation that blesses what the Bible condemns and openly promotes the gay lifestyle as perfectly normal.

The roots of the Kirk and Madsen strategy are taking hold at the very center of our core values. Like the roots of a tree, it is spreading into every area of our society.

It is Taking Root in the Educational System

As early as 1989, renowned Christian educator Dr. Samuel Blumenthal said the following to a group of educators on the state of the educational system, "Christian parents, it is high time to get your children out of public schools. I used to counsel working within the system as active parents, but I am here to tell you the public school system is now so corrupt, you now need to just pull your children out."[13]

The gay agenda strategy will use every opportunity to promote and push for acceptance among adolescents and children. It is much easier to form impressions in a young mind than it is to convince those who have already made up their minds that homosexuality is sexual perversion at its worst. What we're seeing is a more aggressive approach, almost to the point of force-feeding children as young as kindergarten age, under the guise of "anti-bullying, tolerance, and safe school initiatives."

To get some indication of just how far the Obama administration would go to promote the homosexual lifestyle as normal, all you have to do is look at who he appointed as deputy assistant secretary of education in July 2009. To the shock and amazement of many, the president nominated a man by the name of Kevin Jennings as deputy assistant secretary of education in charge of the "Safe and Drug-Free Schools" program.

On the surface the program sounds like something that is much needed in the public school system, however, one of the tenets of the program is to create public schools that are "safe" for homosexual children thus spreading pro-homosexual material (propaganda) throughout the public school system.

"Granted, homosexual propaganda in our schools has become common place, but the appointment of Jennings ensures that for the first time ever, the Federal government will be funding and promoting homosexual propaganda on a large scale basis. This nomination makes clear that President Obama believes America's public school children should be exposed to deviant sexual lifestyles having nothing to do with academics."[14]

It should not surprise anyone to find out that this new appointee is the founder, and until just recently the president, of Gay, Lesbian, Straight Education Network (a.k.a. GLSEN), which is the leading organization working to place homosexual material into the public school system. An objective of their program is to create homosexual "clubs" on all college, high school and middle school campuses.

As an aside, it is interesting to note that when the Supreme Court ruled on gay marriage in 2015, the White House was covered in "rainbow colors" celebrating the disastrous ruling. It only took a few hours to light it up, but it took 5 days for flags to be lowered at half-staff in honor of the four Marines murdered in my hometown of Chattanooga, Tennessee!

Concerning the Supreme Court decision to allow same-sex marriage, Chief Justice John Roberts said, "If you are among the many Americans—of whatever sexual orientation—who favor expanding same-sex marriage, by all means celebrate today's decision... But do not celebrate the Constitution. It had nothing to do with it."[15]

Another example is found in a new and aggressive approach to promote "gender identity" in the Family Life Curriculum of the public school system. Recently in Fairfax County, Virginia, the school board approved lessons about homosexuality and gender identity in a surprising 10-2 vote.

According to the Fairfax County School board website, "The early elementary program emphasizes the importance of families, distinction between good and bad touch, sources of help, and the importance of friendships. Human sexuality is first introduced in grade four. In middle school, students will build "on information learned in late elementary and physiology as well as the physical, psychological and social changes that occur during adolescence. Ninth and tenth graders will be provided definitions for heterosexual, homosexual, bisexual, and transgender and that persons deserve to be treated with respect regardless of their sexual orientation or gender identity."[16]

Many parents voiced opposition to the new curriculum because they were concerned they would not have the "opt out option," because the lessons were moved from the Family Life Curriculum into the mandatory health classes.

What did this mean for parents? They see the move forcing them to do something they do not want to do, which is forcing their children to be exposed to issues that are not even part of the state requirements.

I can remember a time when we used to say, "It's 11:00 PM, do you know where your child is?" But today we are more likely to say it is 11:00 AM, do you know what your child is being taught?"

Below is a brief sampling of the new Common Core State Standards that more than 40 states have adopted, along with politically and morally-based lessons and teaching resources.

- Rejection of religious and moral values
- Pro-evolution, anti-creationism
- Promoting racial ideologies/class warfare

• Promotion of globalism over national sovereignty
• Anti-Second Amendment (promoting a ban on guns)
• Anti-Americanism, anti-capitalism
• Pro-Islamic indoctrination including direct involvement of organizations with close ties to Islamic terrorists/terrorist organizations
• Pro-homosexual, bi-sexual and transgender
• Explicit sex education – some with instruction on how to perform various sex acts including homosexual sex
• Presenting the theory of global warming as fact

It is Taking Root in the Entertainment Industry

It is almost superfluous to say that many Hollywood celebrities, producers and writers have supported and promoted the gay agenda for at least 4 decades. Using the "celebrity influence factor" to promote the homosexual lifestyle as normal is a part of the strategy to swing public opinion in its favor.

Below is a brief illustration of the Entertainment industry's influence on society:

• Homosexual advocacy on television first began to manifest itself in the 1970's.
• In 1972, a made for TV movie "That Certain Summer" featured Hal Holbrook and Martin Sheen as a gay couple.
• In 1973, the reality show "An American Family" featured son Lance Loud's coming out.
• Billy Crystal played a gay character on the ABC sitcom "Soap" in 1977. Despite the fact that the show consistently lost money, ABC kept "Soap" on the air for four seasons.
• Brokeback Mountain was nominated for Best Picture for its unabashedly sympathetic portrayal of a doomed gay relationship.
• Newt Gingrich's half-sister officiated at a gay wedding on "Friends" in the 1990s.
• Late night talk show host, Conan O'Brian, officiated at an ac-

tual gay wedding.

- "Ellen," featuring lesbian Ellen DeGeneres, created a stir when she "came out" on air.
- "Will and Grace" featured a gay man and a straight woman rooming together.
- Fox's musical comedy "Glee" is on the front lines of homosexual advocacy, showing gay sex and slamming anti-gay bullying.
- Other popular shows prominently featuring homosexuals include "Grey's Anatomy" and "Modern Family."
- The ABC drama, "Scandal" features the Chief of Staff as a gay man, who actually got married in the Rose Garden at the White House.
- And, to take the perversion to its logical conclusion, NBC is propagating a false—homosexual—Jesus in its freshman show "Superstore."

It is no wonder that Ben Shapiro declared, in "Primetime Propaganda," that television is the "culture's most ardent advocate for gay marriage."

Hollywood actors and directors have not been shy about their goal to normalize homosexuality. Politicians and journalists who favor homosexuality have also noticed the impact of the entertainment industry on influencing societal attitudes towards homosexuality. In a recent interview in which he came out for homosexual marriage, Vice President Joe Biden declared: "When things really begin to change, is when the social culture changes. I think Will and Grace probably did more to educate the American public [about homosexuality] than almost anything anybody's ever done so far."[17]

It is Taking Root in the Religious Establishment

Mainline denominations are not immune when it comes to the strategy of the gay agenda. As a Bible believing Christian, it is hard for me to fathom how anyone in a denomination that supports same-sex marriage and ordaining gays to the ministry could sit silently in the pew. In fact, denominations that are now openly supporting the gay agenda are losing members by the thousands.

In March 2015, the following headline emblazoned my computer screen, "Presbyterian Church (USA) formally recognized same-sex marriages Tuesday."

The article stated, "On Tuesday, the Presbyterian Church (USA) voted to redefine marriage as 'a commitment between two people, traditionally a man and a woman,' formally allowing same-sex marriages within the church. The vote to modify the church constitution follows last year's recommendation from the church's General Assembly."[18]

Lauren Marohe reported in a March 22, 2015 Huffington Post article that the Presbyterian Church vote was long expected, after 61% of General Assembly delegates voted in June to allow gay and lesbian weddings. That made the 1.8 million-member PCUSA among the largest Christian denominations to take an embracing step toward same-sex marriage."

Listed below are three more mainline denominations which have also succumbed to the gay agenda:

- The Evangelical Lutheran Church of America allows same-sex couples to get married, but leaves it up to individual ministers of congregations to decide, according to a 2009 resolution.
- The Episcopal Church established a rite of blessing for same-sex couples in 2012, and prohibited discrimination against transgender people. Technically, it has no official policy sanctioning same-sex marriage, but it will take up the issue in June.
- The United Church of Christ has allowed same-sex couples to get married since 2005. At the 25th General Synod of the United Church of Christ in Atlanta, it "affirm[ed] equal marriage rights for couples regardless of gender and declares that the government should not interfere with couples regardless of gender who choose to marry and share fully and equally in the rights, responsibilities and commitment of legally recognized marriage."

It was the first major Protestant denomination to do so.[19]

The Demand to Stand for Truth

Instead of the Church of Jesus Christ spreading its influence throughout the culture, just the opposite is actually taking place. After the Supreme Court's landmark ruling on same-sex marriage, some of the leading voices in the evangelical world, men like Franklin Graham and Russell Moore of the Southern Baptist convention, did voice their strong disapproval.

"Yet a smaller but equally impassioned group of evangelicals celebrated the fact that marriage equality is no longer just a dream for LGBT couples across America. It is these leaders who may be pointing to the future of the movement.

About 100 evangelical pastors and leaders signed an online letter published Friday supporting the ruling, and then went one step further by calling on Christians around the country to continue to work for LGBT rights in other areas -- like bullying in schools and employment and housing discrimination."[20]

One of the men who signed the letter is Pastor Danny Cortez of California, who leads the New Heart Community Church. He summed up the feelings of many ministers who have changed their view from one of opposition to one of acceptance, "I believed for years that marriage should only be between one man and one woman," Cortez said. "But as I began relationships with LGBT persons, I saw that my beliefs had been destructive and not in line with the teachings of Jesus Christ. The church doesn't have to fear the positive changes happening in our nation."

The Southern Baptist Convention, the largest Protestant denomination in America, kicked the church out of its fellowship after Cortez changed his views on marriage equality.[21]

There aren't many verses in the Bible that speaks about the sin of homosexuality. But when it does, it condemns it as sin.

You shall not lie with a male as with a woman. It is an abomination.
Leviticus 18:22

If a man lies with a male as he lies with a woman, both of them have committed an abomination. They shall surely be put to death. Their blood shall be upon them.
Leviticus 20:13

For this reason God gave them up to vile passions. For even their women exchanged the natural use for what is against nature. Likewise also the men, leaving the natural use of the woman, burned in their lust for one another, men with men committing what is shameful, and receiving in themselves the penalty of their error which was due . . .
Romans 1:26-27

Do you not know that the unrighteous will not inherit the kingdom of God? Do not be deceived. Neither fornicators, nor idolaters, nor adulterers, nor homosexuals,[a] nor sodomites . . .
1 Corinthians 6:9

. . . knowing this: that the law is not made for a righteous person, but for the lawless and insubordinate, for the ungodly and for sinners, for the unholy and profane, for murderers of fathers and murderers of mothers, for manslayers, for fornicators, for sodomites, for kidnappers, for liars, for perjurers, and if there is any other thing that is contrary to sound doctrine . . .
I Timothy 1:9-10

The only answer to the sin of homosexuality is found in Jesus Christ.

Whoever commits sin also commits lawlessness, and sin is lawlessness. And you know that He was manifested to take away our sins, and in Him there is no sin.
1 John 3:4-5

Our role in society is to speak the truth in love, not to condemn and persecute. Homosexuality is a sin, and like any other sin, it needs to be laid at the cross and forsaken. The Bible says clearly that "all have sinned," homosexual and heterosexual. God will judge our sin, but at the same time He is loving and will forgive us if we repent and receive the salvation available through His dear Son, Jesus.

Don't you see how wonderfully kind, tolerant, and patient God is with you? Does this mean nothing to you? Can't you see that his kindness is intended to turn you from your sin?
Romans 2:4

But anyone who does not love does not know God, for God is love.
1 John 4:8

There is power in the Blood to cleanse from ALL sin!

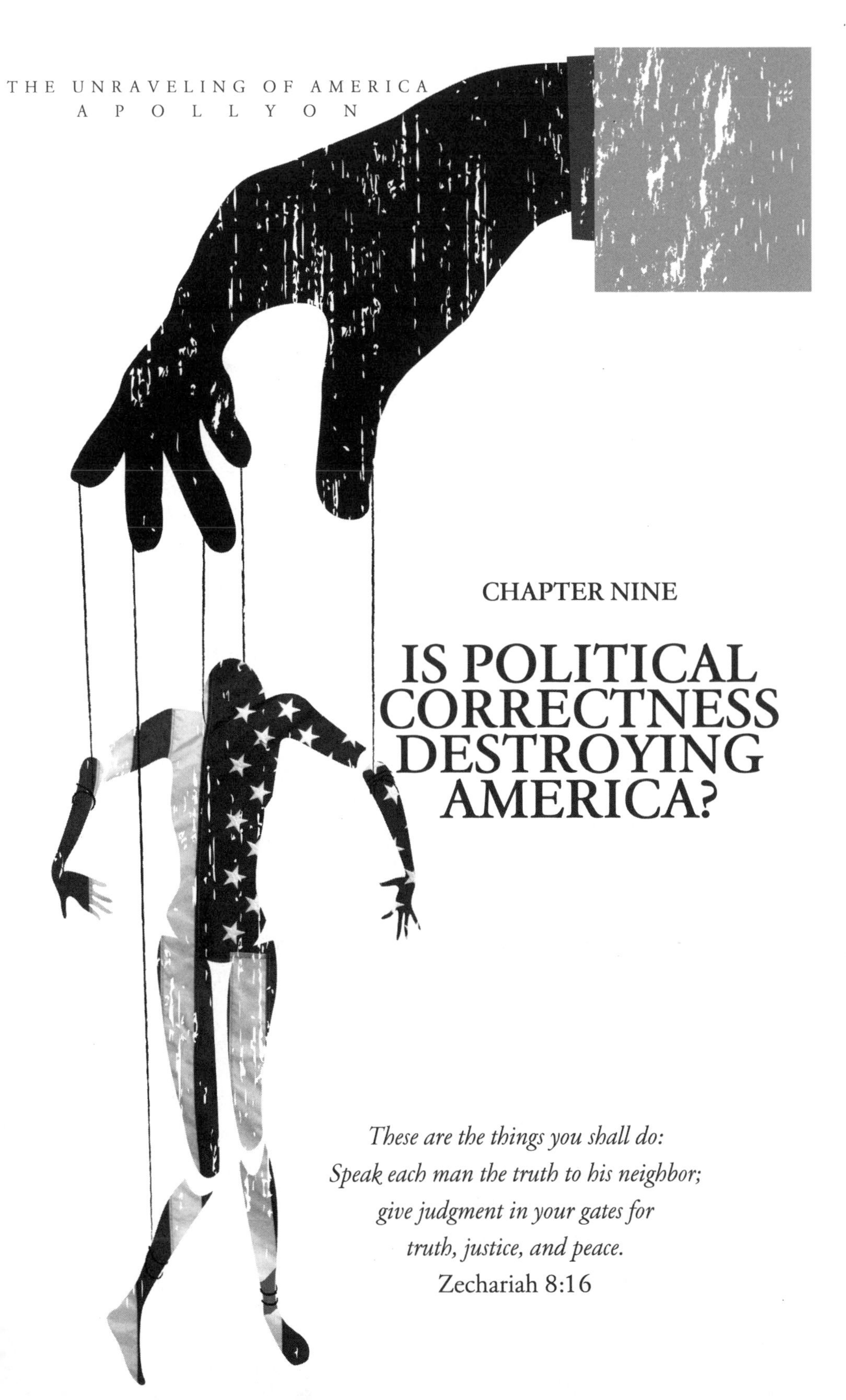

CHAPTER NINE

IS POLITICAL CORRECTNESS DESTROYING AMERICA?

These are the things you shall do:
Speak each man the truth to his neighbor;
give judgment in your gates for
truth, justice, and peace.
Zechariah 8:16

"We are not afraid to entrust the American people with unpleasant facts, foreign ideas, alien philosophies, and competitive values. For a nation that is afraid to let its people judge the truth and falsehood in an open market is a nation that is afraid of its people."
John F. Kennedy[1]

Statistics reveal Americans are fed up with the national news media. The major networks are seeing a steady decline in viewership, print media is losing subscribers by the thousands and the disdain of mainstream media has hit an all time high. Many Americans feel that what they are hearing from the mainstream media is nothing more than regurgitated political correctness in the form of hard-hitting "news."

"A recent Pew Research Center survey found that 65 percent of Americans believe that the national news media have a negative effect on our country. According to a recent Gallup poll, six in ten Americans now have little or no confidence in the national media to report the news fully, accurately and fairly."[2]

A grammar school student by the name of Talha Wani wrote an opinion piece for the *Express Tribune* on the subject, "Can the Media be Trusted?"

He stated, "The media's job is to represent the views and opinions of the masses, and inform and educate people regarding different points of views and opinions. The concept behind the media's role is a simple one: to update society's knowledge on the status of affairs through recent developments and events. Both the print and electronic media have a role to play in this regard. The most rudimentary ethics to follow in this endeavor are honesty and accurate reporting. However, sadly, honesty is the last thing to expect from this now complicated institution.

While the media has the ability to uphold the truth, it has, unfortunately, also been used as a tool of distortion and propaganda, and is often plagued with bias. It often acts as an avenue for profiteering rather than for accurate reporting or creating awareness among the public."[3]

I find it fascinating that a grammar school student sees the seriousness of the situation while those who sit in the comfortable confines of their ivory towers continue dictating to the American public what they should or should not believe. These media moguls don't have a clue that a revolt is taking place in this country. We are fed up and we are not going to take it anymore!

It wasn't always that way.

During the early days of broadcast television, it was not uncommon to turn on the evening news at seven o'clock and watch one of the major networks tell the American people the 'happenings' of the day. For decades, many families ate their evening meal watching Walter Cronkite on CBS or the Huntley/Brinkley report on NBC.

The favorite around our house was Walter Cronkite of CBS news. Because of his straightforward reporting, without mixing his own personal political views, he earned the nickname, "The most trusted man in America." From 1962 to 1991, he reported on some of the most life-changing events in America. With a steadfast voice, he told us the "truth" about the assassination of John F. Kennedy, the death of Martin Luther King and the Vietnam War. Whenever the news broke, he was the one America tuned in to watch.

For decades, we depended on men like Cronkite to give it to us straight and pull no punches. We did not have the luxury of the internet, or the plethora of cable news outlets to get alternative opinions on the events of the day.

In those days, when someone like Walter Cronkite looked into the camera and said, "And that's the way it is," you felt like he was telling you the unvarnished truth.

After the death of Walter Cronkite in 2009, Cliff Kincaid, Director of the Accuracy in Media Center for Investigative Journalism, wrote an article in *Accuracy in Media.* He stated, "It is wrong to speak ill of the dead. On the other hand, it is an insult to the intelligence of the American people to pretend that Walter Cronkite was the "voice of God" and "universally credible," as Mara Liasson put it on Fox News Sunday. The terrible truth is that Walter Cronkite symbolized liberal media bias and used that bias with disastrous consequences for our nation and the world.

We found out after his retirement that he was not only a liberal, which was evident from his broadcasts, but a "one-worlder." In appearances before the World Federalist Association, which favors world government financed by global taxes, he called for the U.S. to renounce "some of its sovereignty" and pass a series of United Nations treaties-many of which are now being pushed in the Senate by President Barack Obama. Cronkite called for an "international Liberty Bell."[4]

I quote Kincaid's article only to illustrate what many of us are now understanding with more clarity. The mainstream media is predominantly comprised of progressive liberals who want to shape the attitudes and opinions of the American public.

My purpose is not to smear or denigrate the good name of Walter Cronkite or anyone else who reported the news during those days. My goal is to simply point out that there was a time in our history when those who reported the news were trusted. Quite frankly, we did not have any idea of their political beliefs or motives. We just viewed the broadcast and print media as unbiased sources, free from personal opinion and ideology.

Remember, it was only a little over 40 years ago that two young reporters by the name of Woodward and Bernstein brought down the President of the United States. These two Washington Post reporters risked their own lives and reputations to give us the facts of the Watergate break-in and subsequent cover-up by the White House.

Americans need the truth, the whole truth, and nothing but the truth. Instead, we are being force fed a steady stream of political correctness by the mainstream media that is facilitating the rhetoric of the progressive liberal agenda, and destroying this nation.

Is Political Correctness Out of Control?

I love the definition of political correctness given by the Urban Dictionary: "The laws of moral and ethical relativism; all systems of cultures and thought are equal in value, stemming from a perceived guilt from white liberals who believe that the Western Civilization is the root of all evil to the exclusion of all else: A powerful form of censorship."[5]

Most agree that the modern movement of political correctness began at the University of Wisconsin-Madison, one of the most liberal colleges in the United States. The University of Wisconsin – Madison served as a jumping-off point that spread to other college campuses and ultimately across the full media landscape.

"Political correctness is a liberal degrading of the freedom of speech. George Orwell's book, *1984*, famously incorporated the notion of limiting thought through language. Words or actions that violate political correctness are called politically incorrect.

Political correctness, or PC, also means the alteration of one's choice of words in order to avoid either offending a group of people or reinforcing a stereotype considered to be disadvantageous to the group. More specifically, groups which (or whose putative leaders or other activists) claim some status as systemically oppressed or discriminated against will periodically attempt to change the terms by which they are referred, and demand that society as a whole change its usage of words as well."[6]

New York Times columnist, William Safire (1929–2009), spent years writing and researching the phraseology of political correctness. He discovered it originated in the early twentieth century in communist literature. It wasn't until 1989 that the phraseology exploded.

Safire opined, "Following the arrogance of its originators, the correctness in political correctness only referred to liberally-approved definitions of political suitability; intuitively it was broadly understood that which was politically correct was what belonged to a consensus about egalitarian advancements that had occurred in the twentieth century for use as a basis in the forthcoming new century. The application of its rules was tolerated as a fairly harmless outlet for liberal busybodies. Within a few years, the strictures the phraseology represented began to be abused, and by 1997, usage of the phraseology declined in correspondence to the tarnishing of its reputation."[7]

There are many who have suggested that 2014 was the year when political correctness reached its peak. That year was so ridiculous that comedian Chris Rock announced he would no longer be performing on college campuses complaining that everything seemed to offend his audiences. You know it's getting bad when a progressive liberal takes issue with political correctness!

In 2014 Americans saw the following:

- In February, Facebook increased its gender list from two – male and female – to 50, including "pangender," "cisgender" and "intersex." In June, after integration with the firm's US gender policy, that figure soared to 71, including "two-spirit person". On February 26, 2015 a Facebook Diversity post announced they expanded the gender options to include a Free Form Field for individuals who do not identify with the extensive list of options.
- In July, white, male superhero Thor became a gender bender, too, when he morphed into the "Female God of Thunder".
- In August, Zara was forced to withdraw an "anti-Semitic" sheriff's T-shirt after a solitary blogger pointed out it looked "simi-

lar" to striped garments that Jews were forced to wear during the Holocaust.

• In October, a billboard ad for the new Mini captioned "topless or bootylicious?" sent masculinity's wall of shame – Everyday Sexism – into overdrive, with users baying for Mini to "sack your entire marketing team for blatant sexism!"

• In November, a "multicultural Christmas jumper" that represents Christianity, Islam, Hinduism, Sikhism and atheism went on sale.[8]

College Campuses Have Become the "Epicenter" of Political Correctness

The PC police are now patrolling the halls of learning in our colleges and universities. What started at the University of Wisconsin – Madison is now the common theme being heard by today's students whose sensitivities require "safe spaces" and "worry free environments."

Since the early 60's, there has been an ongoing effort to redefine the social roles that were traditionally assigned to masculine and feminine identities. All across the landscape of American universities and colleges, liberal/progressive teachers and professors began to impose their politically correct views regarding any recognition of the differences between genders, religious beliefs, sexual orientation, and nationality. Firing the first shot was the feminist movement that demanded the neutral pronouns he, him, and his be replaced with expressions like "he or she," "him or her," and "them," etc.

Little did we know what started in the 60s would morph into what we are seeing now in the twenty-first century. Conservative scholar Robert Bork has charged that the educational system is a battleground, where the future of America is being undermined and ill-served. He has counseled against the troubles which will ensue as a result of anti-religious policies in the schools, permissive attitudes toward homosexuality and abortion, as well as welfare policies that have destroyed families since Lyndon B. Johnson's War on Poverty.[9]

"The truth is that American universities are among the safest and most coddled environments ever devised by man. The idea that one should attend college to be protected from ideas one might find controversial or offensive could only occur to someone who had jettisoned any hope of acquiring an education." - Roger Kimball[10]

In responding to an incident at his university, Dr. Michael S. Roth, President of Wesleyan University, wrote a post on his blog saying that he is tired of hearing complaints about student protesters on college campuses demanding racial and social justice.

Here is a brief excerpt of what he had to say, "Are you sick of reading about pampered college students and their safe spaces, trigger warnings and coddled minds? I know I am. Generations of parents and grandparents have long loved to shake their heads at the apparent absurdities of the young.

It's practically an American tradition: our founding fathers shook their heads about dueling and drinking on campus. When I was a college student, oldsters questioned my generation's patriotism and work ethic. Now my graying generation (with plenty of coloring) questions whether the young people of today have grown too sensitive, and, of course, whether they are ready to take on the world of work that we have prepared for them.

What do pundits mean when they say that students have grown too sensitive? They usually refer to some isolated incident when students become enraged by what seems a minor provocation, like an e-mail from a university administrator about Halloween or about fitting in. But why not turn the question back on the carping columnists? Given the grave issues facing the world, why are pundits so focused on the micro issue of protests on college campuses?"[11]

Dr. Everett Piper, President of Oklahoma Wesleyan University, also had something to say about political correctness when confronted by a student who was upset after a recent chapel service.

He stated in part: "This past week, I actually had a student come forward after a university chapel service and complain because he felt "victimized" by a sermon on the topic of 1 Corinthians 13. It appears this young scholar felt offended because a homily on love made him feel bad for not showing love. In his mind, the speaker was wrong for making him, and his peers, feel uncomfortable.

I'm not making this up. Our culture has actually taught our kids to be this self-absorbed and narcissistic. Any time their feelings are hurt, they are the victims. Anyone who dares challenge them and, thus, makes them "feel bad" about themselves, is a "hater," a "bigot," an "oppressor," and a "victimizer."

So here's my advice: Oklahoma Wesleyan is not a "safe place," but rather, a place to learn: to learn that life isn't about you, but about others; that the bad feeling you have while listening to a sermon is called guilt; that the way to address it is to repent of everything that's wrong with you rather than blame others for everything that's wrong with them. This is a place where you will quickly learn that you need to grow up."[12]

Below are 9 examples of ridiculously PC moments in 2015 that actually occurred on college campuses.

1. In Swarthmore College's student newspaper, hating "pumpkin-spice lattes" was declared sexist.
2. At the University of New Hampshire, the word "American" was declared offensive and should not be used.
3. According to researchers from Idaho State University, College of the Canyons and the Center for Positive Sexuality in Los Angeles, we have to accept people who "identify as real vampires."
4. According to the "Just Words" campaign at the University of Wisconsin–Milwaukee, the phrase "politically correct" was deemed to be politically incorrect.
5. The University of California–Merced blamed a student's clear act of terrorism on the patriarchy.
6. At Quinnipiac University, a sorority had to cancel a

fundraiser for foster children because one student complained that having maracas on the promotional posters was racist.

7. A student at Sonoma State University was ordered to take off a cross that she was wearing because someone "could be offended".

8. North Carolina State University defended a lecturer's right to dock students' grades for using "he" or "him" to refer to both men and women — as well as for using the word "mankind" instead of "humankind."

9. Earlier this year, a Florida Atlantic University student that refused to stomp on the name of Jesus was banned from class.

Just when you thought you had heard everything, there is this from Western Washington University,

An article Josh Logue posted on Inside Higher Ed reports, "One recurring feature of the student protests that have recently swept across college campuses is lists of demands. Add to the list Western Washington University, a public university with about 15,000 students. Late last year, Western made the news after the president called off classes in light of anonymous threats sent via the social media app Yik Yak. Now a student group there calling itself the Student Assembly for Power and Liberation has sent a list of far-reaching demands to the university's president after criticizing the administration for an inadequate response to threats.

The list comprises some of the most expansive -- and resource heavy -- demands put to a university's administration. Among them:

• The list calls for a new building to house the college and that the Student Assembly for Power and Liberation have "direct input and decision-making power over the hiring of faculty for the college."

• The creation of a 15-person student committee called the Office for Social Transformation "to monitor, document and archive all racist, anti-black, transphobic, cissexist, misogynistic, ableist, homophobic, Islamophobic and otherwise oppressive behavior on campus."

• Using a three-strike system, the committee would have the power to take disciplinary action up to and including dismissal against faculty members who receive citations for creating "an unsafe classroom environment."

• And finally, that the university provide tuition reimbursement to "any Western Washington University student who has been targeted by, harassed by or has experienced excruciating acts of violence that [were] racialized, sexualized, gendered, based on ability, employment status, citizenship and/or mental health from the university."[13]

Western Washington University's president, Bruce Shepard, was not totally on board with the list of demands. He cited numerous issues that would be in conflict with policies, practices and mutually agreed contracts, but did leave the final decision up to the faculty Senate and student government. It will certainly be interesting to see how this turns out.

Political Correctness Gone Wild in the Marketplace

The mainstream media feels an obligation to its audiences to bombard the airwaves with messages about what they consider appropriate speech. Sometimes these messages are blatant, at other times very subtle. Sadly, most of the time, we fall for the deception and subscribe to an unwritten speech code without giving it much thought.

Those who choose not to do so are discovering the dire consequences of challenging the system.

Michael Snyder gave the following seven examples of what is transpiring in America beyond our universities, in his 2013 article:

1. The Missouri State Fair has permanently banned a rodeo clown from performing just because he wore an Obama mask, and now all of the other rodeo clowns are being required to take "sensitivity training"

2. Government workers in Seattle have been told that they should no longer use the words "citizen" and "brown bag" because they are potentially offensive.
3. The mayor of Washington D.C. recently asked singer Donnie McClurkin not to attend a Martin Luther King, Jr. memorial concert because of his views on homosexuality.
4. The governor of California has signed a bill into law which will allow transgendered students to use whatever bathrooms and gym facilities that they would like . . . Since then President Obama has endorsed the federal guidlines established by the US Department of Education requiring public schools to allow transgender students to use restrooms and locker rooms that correspond to their gender of choice.
5. In San Francisco, authorities have installed small plastic "privacy screens" on library computers so that perverts can continue to exercise their "right" to watch pornography at the library without children being directly exposed to it.
6. According to a new Army manual, U.S. soldiers will now be instructed to avoid "any criticism of pedophilia" and to avoid criticizing "anything related to Islam".
7. The Obama administration has banned all U.S. government agencies from producing any training materials that link Islam with terrorism. In fact, the FBI has gone back and purged references to Islam and terrorism from hundreds of old documents.[14]

He went on to say, "When Americans go to work or go to school, the conversations that they have with others are mostly based on content that the media feeds them. And about 90 percent of what we watch on television is controlled by just six gigantic corporations. The establishment wants to control what we say and how we think, and they have a relentless propaganda machine that never stops working."[15]

The Bible tells us that Satan is the "prince of the power of the air" (Ephesians 2:2). Controlling information through the use of airwaves is nothing new, it's been going on since the Garden of Eden. It would be a fatal mistake to underestimate the power that is wielded by the mainstream media over the thoughts, words and actions of the American public. The spirit of antichrist is at work behind the scenes pulling the strings in an attempt to reshape our worldview to better conform to a more progressive/anti-Biblical society. It appears to be working!

Coming to a Church Near You

Just how far will this go? I do not know the answer to that. But, one thing I do know is that God's people must stand up and speak the truth of God's Word or we will see the pressure of the progressive agenda grow to the point where even the pulpits of America will be silenced. You may think that will never happen in America! I don't want to shock you, but it is already happening.

Recently in Houston, Texas, controversial mayor Annise Parker, tried to subpoena church sermons, along with other documentation, from five local pastors. Why would she do that? City officials wanted to know what these preachers were saying about homosexuality and other gender issues that they deemed divisive to the greater community, and contrary to a recently passed ordinance. These faith leaders were vehemently opposed to a controversial equal rights ordinance proposed by the mayor and the city council.

"According to the Houston Chronicle, the subpoenas, which were issued last month, seek, "all speeches, presentations, or sermons related to HERO, the Petition, Mayor Annise Parker, homosexuality, or gender identity prepared by, delivered by, revised by, or approved by you or in your possession." Parker, a lesbian, is the first openly gay mayor of a major U.S. city, as Religion News Services noted."

The move comes as the city of Houston is defending itself against a lawsuit brought by local activists and pastors who are seeking the suspension of the controversial ordinance.

The pastors who have had their sermons subpoenaed are not parties in the lawsuit, though they are part of a coalition of more than 400 preachers and churches in the Houston area who are opposed to portions of the city's non-discrimination ordinance. The ordinance, which passed in May, has been debated for months, as the new regulations would allow transgendered individuals to file complaints if they are denied restroom usage and would ban discrimination in both business and housing.

In a city document produced earlier this year to explain the purpose of the ordinance, Houston officials argued that the city is desperately in need of increased protections based on both "sexual orientation" and "gender identity."[16]

Do ministers not have the right to speak out on social issues based on the constitutional provisions of the First Amendment? In 2012, a large number of pastors from across all 50 states decided to take a stand. They did so in defiance of the IRS rules and regulations that prohibit preaching sermons on the political positions of electoral candidates from a biblical perspective.

The news report stated, a total of 1,586 pastors participated in Pulpit Freedom Sunday in all 50 states, the District of Columbia, and Puerto Rico. In so doing, they exercised their constitutionally protected freedom to engage in religious expression from the pulpit despite an Internal Revenue Service rule known as the *Johnson Amendment* that activist groups often use to silence churches by threatening their tax-exempt status.

"'Pastors should decide what they preach from the pulpit, not the IRS,' said Senior Legal Counsel Erik Stanley. 'It's outrageous for pastors and churches to be threatened or punished by the government for applying biblical teachings to all areas of life, including candidates and elections. The question is, 'who should decide the content of sermons: pastors or the IRS?'"

But pastors who participate in Pulpit Freedom Sunday are not engaging in a 'political crusade.' Instead, they are simply applying

Scripture and theological doctrine to the positions held by the candidates running for office. Pastors have been applying scriptural teaching to circumstances facing their congregations for centuries. This is not 'political' speech. Rather, it's core religious expression from a spiritual leader to his congregants. That kind of expression is at the very center of the freedom of speech and religion protections in the First Amendment.

The real question is this: When has the government ever been allowed to condition any government-recognized status (such as tax-exempt status) on the surrender of a constitutionally protected freedom?"[17]

The Gospel Is Not (and never will be) Politically Correct

In the perfect politically correct world, no group or individual would ever be offended in any way. Do not misunderstand, I do not believe that Christians should say things to hurt or demean anyone. However, the truth of the Gospel, by its very definition, is offensive to the "natural mind" (1 Corinthians 2:6-14).

The Apostle Paul was not politically correct. He made reference to the "offense of the cross" in Galatians 5:11, *"And I, brethren, if I still preach circumcision, why do I still suffer persecution? Then the offense of the cross has ceased."* What was so offensive about the cross? It was offensive to the Jews because they believed salvation was based on works (John 6:28–29). Paul preached salvation was by grace, through faith alone, and that became a stumbling block and an offense to the Jewish mindset (Romans 3:20). All the law-keeping in the world was of no value when it came to salvation.

When Jesus came preaching salvation by grace, He was definitely not considered politically correct. He exploded on the scene with such spiritual force that He shattered their previously held traditions. When it comes to being offended by the work of Jesus on the cross, the Jews were not alone. There are many today who "stumble" over the idea that a person can be saved by trusting in the finished work and the shed blood of Jesus on the cross of Calvary. Just mentioning the fact that you cannot "earn" your way into heaven is a major offense and stumbling block. The message of the cross is just as offensive today as it was in the day that Paul declared it!

It is about time for the church to be more concerned with the fact that millions of people are dying without Jesus Christ than they are with political correctness. Our eternal citizenship is in heaven (Philippians 3:20–21), and we must exemplify citizens and ambassadors of our Heavenly King!

CHAPTER TEN

CONSPIRACY OF SILENCE

(Things the Mainstream Media Doesn't Want You to Know)

And you shall know the truth, and the truth shall make you free.

John 8:32

"Everything we hear is an opinion, not a fact. Everything we see is a perspective, not the truth."
Marcus Aurelius[1]

On April 24, 2015, Hillary Clinton gave her first speech as a presidential candidate for the 2016 election. She made it clear that, if elected president of the United States, she will push for legislation providing unlimited access to abortion. Her remarks were made at the sixth annual Women in the World Summit, a feminist group that shoulders the pro-abortion agenda.

While her progressive viewpoints were not surprising, during the course of her speech she made a statement that caused me to sit up and take notice.

As she continued to rally the crowd, Ms. Clinton said, "deep-seated cultural codes, religious beliefs and structural biases have to be changed for the sake of giving "access" to women for "reproductive health care." The comment was a shot across the bow at pro-life advocates and countries with pro-life laws.[2]

Keep in mind, the stated goal of the socialist/progressive movement is to fundamentally transform America. In order to do that, according to Ms. Clinton, "deep-seated cultural codes, religious beliefs and structural biases have to be changed." So what was she really saying? In order to reshape America, certain "old fashioned" views and other long held beliefs and traditions must be removed.

The real question is this: Is mainstream media a sympathetic "co-conspirator" in promoting and propagating the progressive agenda? To answer that question, you have to ask a second question: Is mainstream media biased against those who hold a strong conservative belief system? Is America receiving a subtle, subversive push toward a progressive agenda at the hand of media reports on the issues of the day?

"Since citizens cannot cast informed votes or make knowledgeable decisions on matters of public policy if the information on which they depend is distorted, it is vital to American democracy that television news and other media be fair and unbiased.

In a recent Gallup Poll, the majority of Americans said they believe that the mass media slant reports in favor of the liberal position on current issues.

[The bias] is not the result of a vast left-wing conspiracy – [there is] an unconscious "groupthink" mentality that taints news coverage and allows only one side of a debate to receive a fair hearing. When that happens, the truth suffers."[3]

According to the Society of Professional Journalist code of ethics published on the spj.org website, "Ethical journalism should be accurate and fair." Journalists are charged in the ethical code to "avoid stereotyping. Journalists should examine the ways their values and experiences may shape their reporting."
(https/www.spj.org/ethicscode.asp) Presenting the facts without injecting opinion, philosophy or ideology should be the goal. As you read, listen or watch the news, how is it possible to know if the reporting is biased? I have discovered biased reporting falls into one of the following categories:

- **Bias by omission** – leaving one side out of an article, or a series of articles over a period of time; bias by omission can occur either within a story, or over the long term as a particular news outlet reports one set of events, but not another.
- **Bias by selection of sources** – including more sources that support one view over another. This bias can also be seen when a reporter uses such phrases as "experts believe," "observers say," or "most people believe."
- **Bias by story selection** – a pattern of highlighting news stories that coincide with the agenda of either the Left or the Right,

while ignoring stories that coincide with the opposing view.

- **Bias by placement** – story placement is a measure of how important the editor considers the story. Studies have shown that, in the case of the average newspaper reader and the average news story, most people read only the headline.
- **Bias by labeling** – bias by labeling comes in two forms: The first is the tagging of conservative politicians and groups with extreme labels while leaving liberal politicians and groups unlabeled or with more mild labels, or vice versa. The second kind of bias by labeling occurs when a reporter not only fails to identify a liberal as a liberal or a conservative as a conservative, but describes the person or group with positive labels, such as "an expert" or "independent consumer group."
- **Bias by spin** – bias by spin occurs when the story has only one interpretation of an event or policy, to the exclusion of the other; spin involves tone – it's a reporter's subjective comments about objective facts; makes one side's ideological perspective look better than another.[4]

The "Progressive" Billionaire Who is Really Pulling the Strings

The billionaire I am talking about is not Donald Trump! To better understand any movement, it is helpful to look at its leaders. In the progressive camp there is no one more influential than George Soros.

He isn't running for office. He does not sit in the Senate, nor does he offer legislation in the House of Representatives. Some have called him the "puppet master," pulling the strings to move America toward the progressive agenda.

Who is George Soros? He was born August 12, 1930. He is of Jewish-Hungarian ancestry and holds dual citizenship (Hungary and the United States). He is best known as the chairman of Soros Fund Management. He became known as "The Man Who Broke the Bank of England" because of his reported short sale of $10 billion (US) worth of pounds, resulting in a profit of $1 billion during the 1992 Black Wednesday UK currency crisis. He is on the list of the 30 richest people in the world, and has reportedly dedicated much of his fortune to push a progressive agenda.

Human Events, a conservative "think tank", asked its readers who they considered the most dangerous progressive leader in America. Far and away they chose George Soros.

Below is an excerpt from the article "Top Ten Reasons This Man is Dangerous," compiled by Human Events:

1. **Gives billions to left-wing causes:** Soros started the Open Society Institute in 1993 as a way to spread his wealth to progressive causes. Using Open Society as a conduit, Soros has given more than $7 billion to a who's who of left-wing groups.
2. **Influence on U.S. elections:** Soros once said that removing President George W. Bush from office in 2004 was the "central focus of my life." His early financial support helped jump-start Barack Obama's political career.
3. **Wants to curtail American sovereignty:** He wants more power for groups such as the World Bank and International Monetary Fund, even while saying the U.S. role in the IMF should be "downsized."
4. **Media Matters:** Soros is a financial backer of Media Matters for America, a progressive media watchdog group that hyperventilates over any conservative view that makes it into the mainstream media.
5. **MoveOn.org:** Soros has been a major funder of MoveOn.org, a progressive advocacy group and political action committee that raises millions for liberal candidates.
6. **Center for American Progress:** Headed by John Podesta, White House chief of staff under President Clinton, the Center for American Progress has been instrumental in providing progressive talking points and policy positions for the Obama administration.

7. Environmental extremism: Former Obama green jobs czar Van Jones and his leftist environmental ideas have been funded by Soros' money at these groups: the Ella Baker Center, Green For All, the Center for American Progress, and the Apollo Alliance, which was instrumental in getting $110 billion in green initiatives included in Obama's stimulus package.

8. America Coming Together: Soros gave nearly $20 million to this "527 group" with the express purpose of defeating President Bush.

9. Currency manipulation: A large part of Soros' multibillion-dollar fortune has come from manipulating currencies. During the 1997 Asian financial crisis, Malaysian Prime Minister Mahathir bin Mohamad accused him of bringing down the nation's currency through his trading activities, and in Thailand he was called an "economic war criminal."

10. Delusions: Soros has repeatedly said that he sees himself as a messianic figure. "I admit that I have always harbored an exaggerated view of my self-importance—to put it bluntly, I fancied myself as some kind of god" or "I carried some rather potent messianic fantasies with me from childhood, which I felt I had to control, otherwise I might end up in the loony bin."

As it is, one of the wealthiest men in the world is using his billions to impose a radical agenda on America.[5]

Looking at both sides of any issue is the only way to be fair and balanced. I am of the opinion there are certain "hot button issues" that the mainstream media is refusing to give a complete accounting so the American public can make up its own mind.

There are at least three topics where I challenge the "fair-and-balanced" nature of reporting.

1. Global Warming

Is global warming a settled fact or sloppy science? I believe in climate change. I live in East Tennessee where if you don't like the climate now, wait fifteen minutes and it will change. Seriously, climate change has occurred since the beginning of creation. But that is not the real issue with the science of global warming. It is more about money and power than it is about a clean planet. I am afraid that global warming has become a political football more than settled science.

On one side of the issue are global warming skeptics, like John Coleman, who said, "It is the greatest scam in history. I am amazed, appalled and highly offended by it. Global Warming; It is a scam. Some dastardly scientists with environmental and political motives manipulated long term scientific data to create an illusion of rapid global warming."[6]

Yet, there are many defenders such as Diane Feinstein, liberal senator from California, who said, "Global warming is real. It is happening today. It is being charted by our satellites. It is being charted by our scientists. It is being charted by those of us in this body, and I think the real key is if we are ready to admit that fact and take the action to make the necessary conversion."[7]

The religion of global warming ascended to new heights when President Obama linked climate instability to terrorism. During his State of the Union message he suggested, "No challenge poses a greater threat to future generations than climate change."[8]

In another interview Obama said, "What we know is that — as human beings are placed under strain, then bad things happen. And, you know, if you look at world history, whenever people are desperate, when people start lacking food, when people — are not able to make a living or take care of their families — that's when ideologies arise that are dangerous."[9]

An entire industry has been created to pump billions of dollars into the spread of global warming information - or as some call it, propaganda - into society. Again, it seems the mainstream media has participated with only a one-sided push of the issue - mankind is responsible for global warming. If you dare speak in opposition to global warming, you are labeled as a "climate change denier" and put in the category with someone who would deny the Holocaust ever happened.

Did you know that just recently Attorney General Lynch told the Senate Judiciary Committee "that not only has she discussed internally the possibility of pursuing civil actions against so-called 'climate change deniers,' but she has 'referred' it to the FBI to consider whether or not it meets the criteria for which we could take action."[10]

"Lynch was responding to a question from Sen. Sheldon Whitehouse, D-R.I., who urged Lynch to prosecute those who 'pretend that the science of carbon emissions' dangers is unsettled,' particularly those in the 'fossil fuel industry' who supposedly have constructed a 'climate denial apparatus.' Lynch is apparently following in the footsteps of California Attorney General Kamala Harris and New York Attorney General Eric Schneiderman, both of whom have opened up investigations of ExxonMobil for allegedly lying to the public and their shareholders about climate change.

None of the public officials involved in this abuse of the prosecutorial power of the government recognize the outrageousness of what they are doing, or are urging the FBI and the Justice Department to do. They want to investigate and prosecute corporations and individuals for their opinions on an unproven scientific theory, for which there is not a consensus, despite inaccurate claims to the contrary.

This not only represents a serious blow against the free flow of ideas and the vigorous debate over scientific issues that is a hallmark of an advanced, technological society like ours, it is a fundamental violation of the First Amendment. Will the FBI's possible investigation include going after dissenting scientists who publish articles or give speeches questioning the global climate change hypothesis?"[11]

Could questioning the reliability of climate change data or rhetoric cause you to land on the opposite side of the federal government? According to a newsweek.com article originally published on cato.com, Senator Whitehouse (D-RI) has urged the U.S. to use the RICO law enacted to catch Mafia dons, to file a racketeering suit against oil and coal industries and "conservative policy groups" that "have promoted wrongful thinking on climate change." So much for the First Amendment!

We are close to a totalitarian regime that will go to any length to silence its critics. Allowing the free flow of ideas and honest debate is the only way a FREE society can remain FREE.

2. Black Lives Matter

The "Black Lives Matter" movement became a nationally known phenomenon following the killing of a 17-year-old black teenager in Ferguson, Missouri. The original purpose of the movement was to bring national attention to a perceived racial bias in the criminal justice system, claiming that a disproportionate number of black individuals are routinely killed by white police officers. However, not everyone agrees. There are many in the law enforcement community, and among conservative leaders, that feel if they voice an opposite view, the mainstream media will simply ignore it at best, or label them detractors, racist and bigots at worst!

The question becomes, what is the more appropriate phrase: black lives matter, or do all lives matter? The movement maintains they are simply trying to draw attention to the fact that most people don't think their lives matter at all. They suggest it is not because they don't think other lives matter, it is just their lives matter a little bit more. Is that really where we are as a country? Do we have to decide which lives matter more simply based on the color of someone's skin?

Unfortunately, the Black Lives Matter movement is not just about educating the public on racial inequalities. It has morphed into violent extremism that goes beyond holding up signs and marching in the street.

"Actions speak louder than words, and the violent rhetoric BLM spews makes it hard to believe such a defense. Whether it be advocating for the murder of police, or racial segregation, BLM seems intent on reversing the Civil Rights movement, not launching a new one.

We saw BLM protesters (among many other leftist groups) shut down a Trump rally in Chicago, with violence then breaking out. Protesters shattered the windows of cars with Trump stickers, and assaulted police.

If Trump wins the election, BLM has more violence planned. As the DC Gazette reports: Black Lives Matter spokesman, Tef Poe, has always been the voice of the bigoted group. In November 2014, Poe was even flown to the United Nations offices in Geneva, Switzerland to speak about "police violence." Funny, now that very same person is now inciting a race riot. And these folks think asking for an official ID card before voting amounts to intimidation?"[12]

In an August 12, 2015 article on breitbart.com, Jerome Hudson listed five truths he believes are being ignored by the mainstream media and the leadership of the BLM movement:

Truth #1. Planned Parenthood is profiting from the genocide of black babies.

- One would think that the exposure of a taxpayer-funded black genocide would have been the focus of furor from Black America's new civil rights reformers.
- At least 79% of Planned Parenthood's abortion mills are within walking distance of black or Hispanic neighborhoods.
- In New York City in 2009, 47%, or 40,798, of the city's 87,273 abortions, were performed on black women.
- In 2009, nearly half of the black pregnancies in New York City ended in abortion and yet, Times Square was not filled with Black Lives Matter protesters demanding the shuttering of Planned Parenthood's doors. Do those black lives not matter?[13]

Truth #2. There exists a lopsided self-inflicted violence in Black America, and #BlackLivesMatter doesn't address it.

- In 2011, we learned that black males 15-34 were 10 times more likely to die of murder than their white counterparts.
- According to FBI data, 4,906 black people killed other blacks in 2010 and 2011. That is more than the total number of U.S. military deaths in Iraq over the last decade. More black Americans killed other blacks in two years than were lynched from 1882 to 1968, according to the Tuskegee Institute.
- Of course, black people are not unique to intra-racial murder, but a subculture of wanton disregard for human life has consigned so many black neighborhoods to a sort of ceaseless state of despair.[14]

Truth #3. Michael Brown, Eric Garner, and Freddie Gray are not martyrs.

- On the day he died, Michael Brown was a burglary suspect. After a fistfight and a failed attempt to disarm Officer Darren Wilson, Michael Brown was shot dead before he could continue his attack. That he had his "hands up" in surrender is a pernicious lie.
- Eric Garner was committing the "crime" of selling un-taxed cigarettes when he was apprehended by a half-dozen cops. Garner died after being placed in a chokehold by an arresting officer. Ultimately, a Staten Island grand jury concluded that there wasn't enough evidence to bring a criminal indictment against the NYPD officer who killed Eric Garner.
- Freddie Gray died from a severe spinal cord injury while in police custody. He had a penchant for running from the police and a "history," according to the Baltimore Sun, "of participating in 'crash-for-cash' schemes—injuring himself in law enforcement settings to collect settlements."[15]

Truth #4. There is no national conspiracy of police officers to hunt black people.

- The common denominator that connects the deaths of these three men is the fact that they all resisted arrest. None of them deserved death. But they all made terrible decisions that led to their demise.
- Unfortunately, the anti-police Black Lives Matter-led protests that resulted in the rioting, looting, and burning of businesses is desperately uninterested in the truth.
- Even Eric Garner's daughter "doubts" that her father's death was motivated by race. Garner's mother said she would "agree."[16]

Truth #5. We need to be honest with ourselves and face facts.

- Our nation's newspapers feature, with haunting predictably, headline after headline detailing the carnage that has consumed dozens of communities where black men kill each other with terrifying regularity.
- There are no national rallies, no mass media coverage, and no presidential eulogies to call attention to the madness.
- Many of black America's wounds are self-inflicted. So let's broaden the parameters of our discussion about the issues vexing black Americans and press pause on all the political grandstanding and phony posturing about whose lives matter.[17]

Leaders of the BLM continue to reveal the real intent of the movement. Their words unveil their agenda.

BLM co-founder Marissa Jenae Johnson recently stated that the phrase "all lives matter", has now been added to the ever-expanding list of unacceptable phrases. She contends that the phrase is a new "racial slur."

In a recent interview with Fox news national correspondent John Roberts, the 24-year-old Seattle-based activist had more to say, "White Americans have created the conditions that require a phrase like 'Black Likes Matter.' Do you know how horrific it is to grow up as a child in a world that so hates you? While you're literally being gunned down in the street, while you're being rounded up and mass incarcerated and forced into prison slavery."

"Black Lives Matter is not a strong enough statement for me," Johnson added. "What it's gonna take to dismantle white supremacy is white folks actually gotta give up something," she said. "You have to actually sacrifice yourself. You have to be willing to give up the things that you currently benefit from."

It's bizarre to hear the words "white supremacy" seriously uttered in describing the structure of power in America today. Somehow a nation of white supremacists elected a black president – twice![18]

3. The Genocide of Christians.

Does the mainstream media purposely participate in a "conspiracy of silence" when it comes to the reporting of the ongoing genocide of Christians and the wholesale destruction of sacred sites in the Middle East? Some have suggested that it is rather a matter of "blind spots" in reporting the stories of Christians and other minorities that are being persecuted.

An abc.com article by Natasha Moore, reports that Paul Marshall, Lela Gilbert, and Roberta Green-Ahmanson, "The authors of the 2008 book *Blind Spot: When Journalists Don't Get Religion* offer some suggestions. Firstly, they argue that Western journalists on the whole tend to be more secular than their readers, thinking only in terms of 'secular Western preconceptions about oppression, economics, freedom and progress.' Quoting GK Chesterton, they note that secularism is happy to analyze motives in terms of nationality, profession, place of residence, or hobby, but refuses to consider 'the creeds we hold about the cosmos in which we live.' But journalism is radically incomplete without an understanding of the core beliefs of the majority of the earth's population."[19]

Moore states that the authors go on to give an example of why this omission is problematic, "The book cites the reportage of a massacre in the offices of a Karachi charity in 2002 where terrorists picked out and murdered seven Christian workers while sparing their Muslim colleagues. Author Paul Marshall, Senior Fellow at the Hudson Institute's Center for Religious Freedom, observes:

"CNN International contented itself with the opinion that there was 'no indication of a motive'. Would it have said the same if armed men had invaded a multiracial center, separated the black people from the white people, then methodically killed all the blacks and spared all the whites?"[20]

Whether the mainstream media decides to cover the atrocities or not, the fact remains that in the Middle East, the home of Christianity and place where Jesus was born, Christians face daily persecution. There is ample evidence coming from numerous sources that the incidences of daily persecution, beheadings and torture are not fantasy but fact. Often when Christians are captured by Islamic terrorists, they are told to convert to Islam or pay an exorbitant tax. If they refused to convert or couldn't pay, they'd be killed.

The Reverend Franklin Graham of Samaritans Purse recently visited the Middle East and told Megyn Kelly on Fox News about the plight of Christians, "Christians are not only being targeted, but they are being butchered. The women are usually raped by the soldiers. The men are shot or beheaded in front of their families. This takes place every day."[21]

After months of waiting, the U.S. State Department, under President Obama, finally recognized the ongoing genocide. Under mounting pressure, Secretary of State John Kerry finally determined that the Islamic State (ISIS) has committed genocide against Christians and other minority groups such as Yazidis and Shias. "The declaration, while long sought by Congress and human rights groups, changes little," notes The Associated Press (AP). "It does not obligate the United States to take additional action against ISIS militants and does not prejudge any prosecution against its members."[22]

According to CEO David Curry of Open Doors USA, in 2015 Islamic extremism and authoritarian governments combined to produce the worst year in modern history for Christians around the world. "The trend spiked upward in the Middle East, Africa and Central Asia, with thousands of Christians killed or imprisoned, and even more chased from their homes. Islamic extremism continues to be the primary driving force behind the expansion of persecution. It is no longer just a Christian problem, but a global problem that must be addressed."[23]

Tony Perkins of the Family Research Council recently held a news conference that summed up the tragic situation, and pointed out the inaction of the US government in helping Christians in the Middle East. He said, "Our administration has been reluctant to call this what it is and it is genocide, and there's a reason. Because if we recognize what is happening in Syria and Iraq, we then have a moral and legal obligation to do something."[24]

I only covered three issues that I believe are being neglected by the mainstream media. There are others just as important, such as: the truth about marijuana; the ongoing fight over gun rights, and the continual struggle of the church finding her voice to speak to this generation. Let me remind you, Jesus said, "And you shall know the truth, and the truth shall make you free (John 8:32). It is not just the truth that makes you free, but it is the known truth that makes the difference.

Discover the truth for yourself and you will see that we must take a stand. It is one thing to decry what is perceived to be a "conspiracy of silence" by the mainstream media. It is another thing to let your voice be heard, declaring the truth for all to hear.

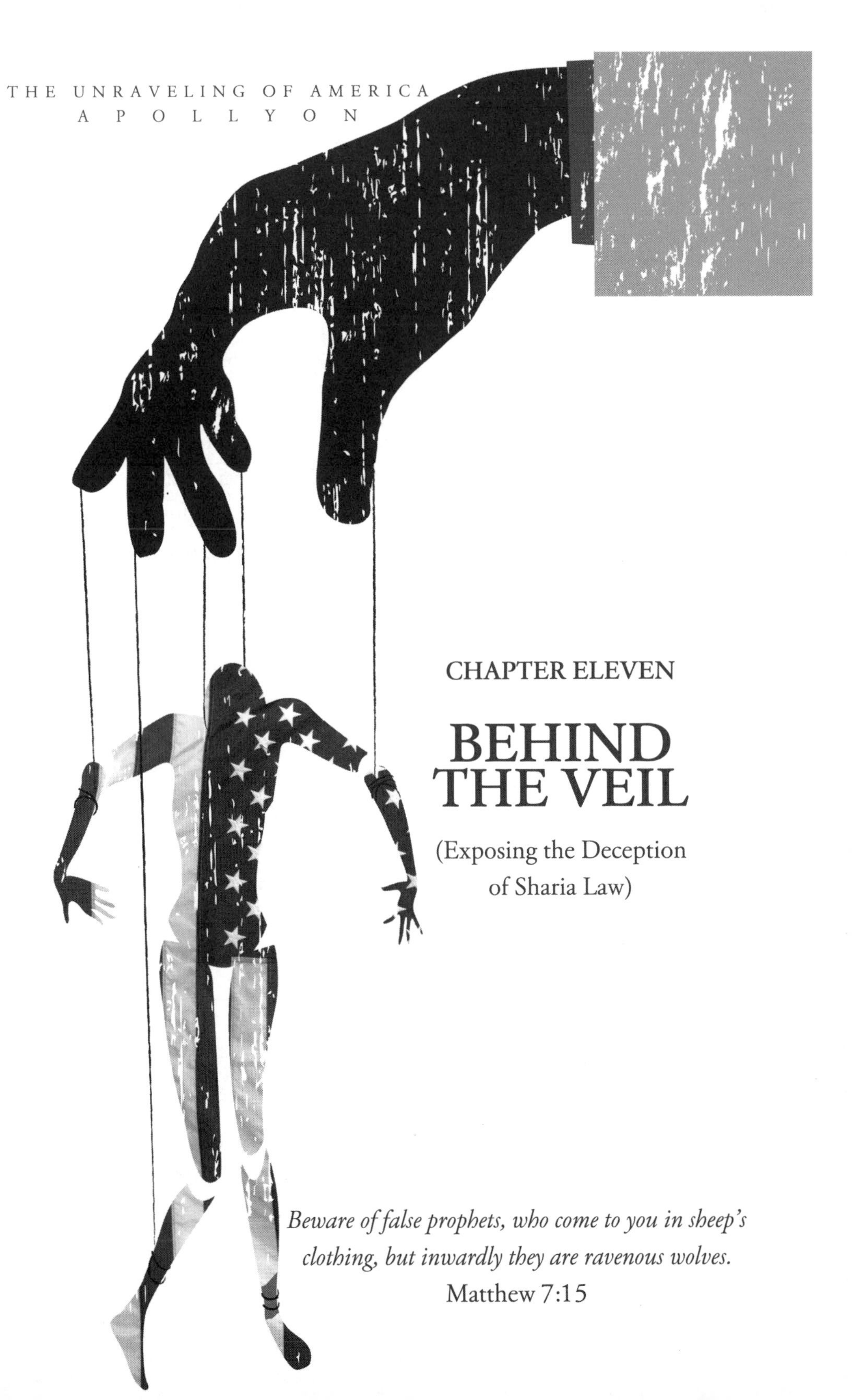

CHAPTER ELEVEN

BEHIND THE VEIL

(Exposing the Deception of Sharia Law)

Beware of false prophets, who come to you in sheep's clothing, but inwardly they are ravenous wolves.
Matthew 7:15

"We are used to facing the United States as a fortress from the outside. Now we are finding a breach to penetrate the country (the U.S.) and confront it from within."
Muammar Kaddafi[1]

"So we want an Islamic State where Islamic law is not just in the books but enforced, and enforced with determination. There is no space and no room for democratic consultation. The Shari'ah is set and fixed, so why do we need to discuss it anymore? Just implement it!"
Abu Bakar Bashir[2]

Several years ago George Barna wrote a book, *"The Frog in the Kettle."* He used an interesting title designed to remind us how easy it is to, slowly and gradually, drift into a major "pot of trouble." The title comes from an old fable about the best way to cook a frog.

The parable told us if you just throw a frog into a pot of boiling water, it will leap out and hop away from danger. But, if you put that same frog into a pot that is filled with cold water, he's perfectly comfortable. Slowly you increase the heat, and before he realizes what is going on, he's cooked. The hot water saps his strength and he becomes powerless to jump out.

Scientists have disproven this theory, however the cultural analogy of slow change destroying or overtaking society has been tried and tested throughout history. It does remind us how gradually bad things can happen if we don't pay attention to the temperature change.

The Slow Boil Has Begun

Little by little, we are finding ourselves as a country being 'warmed up' to some very serious issues. America and Western Europe are warming the water of Islamic extremism. Each day brings new threats and overt acts of terrorism to remind us that a day of reckoning is fast approaching. Every time a new terrorist attack takes place and our elected leaders refuse to acknowledge the facts, we turn our backs on the truth and the temperature is increased another degree!

Consider the attack by radical Islamic terrorists in Brussels, killing at least 30 innocents, and wounding over 300 people. Among the killed and wounded were at least five American citizens. In the meantime, the leader of the free world was attending a baseball game in Cuba with communist leader Raul Castro. Instead of hopping on Air Force One and heading back to Washington, D.C. to monitor the crisis, or flying to Brussels, Belgium to stand with the leaders of a broken country, he chose to do the "wave" with Castro. During an interview with ESPN, one of the hosts at the game asked Obama how he could sit and enjoy the game after such a devastating attack, "It's always a challenge when you have a terrorist attack anywhere in the world, particularly of this age of 24/7 news coverage. You want to be respectful and understand the gravity of the situation, but the whole premise of terrorism is to try to disrupt people's ordinary lives,"[3] commented President Obama.

His rationale is that if we change our daily lives, the terrorists win. Now on the surface that is a logical argument. But, what I see is an ongoing and consistent pattern of denial that refuses to acknowledge that Islamic terrorism is not just an isolated event occurring to scare people. These horrific events are part of an overall plan to subjugate 'unbelievers' under the boot of radical Islam by any means necessary.

In reflecting on the Brussels bombing, Ann Corcoran, at Refugee Resettlement Watch, wrote, "There is only one difference between us and them (Europe), they have been seeing the colonization longer and the percentage of the Muslim population is higher than ours is here in America. How can our 'leaders' possibly not see the same future for us if we allow the Muslim population to continue to grow exponentially?"[4]

Europe allowed more than a million migrants and refugees to enter the continent on November 15, 2015, up from 280,000 in 2014. According to a washingtontimes.com article, The Associated Press reported that President Barack Obama intends to bring in 10,000 Syrian refugees to the U.S. in fiscal year 2016 – five times the number resettled in the past four years. About 98 percent of the Syrian refugees are Muslim.

Behind the Veil - What is Sharia Law?

Most Americans know very little about Islam, and less about Sharia Law. We have been fed a story line that is something of a fairy tale when it comes to really understanding the Muslim agenda. Over one hundred years ago, Sir William Muir, a Scottish born scholar of Islam and colonial administrator said, "The sword of Muhammad and the Qur'an (Koran) are the most fatal enemies of civilization, truth and liberty which the world has yet known."[5]

Islam is a political system with its own body of laws called Sharia. Sharia law is based on entirely different principles than our laws in America. Many of these laws concern the non-Muslims. Every demand that Muslims make move us one step closer to the goal of implementing Sharia law in America. Islamic followers claim their law is perfect, universal and eternal. They claim the laws of the United States (the Constitution) are temporary, limited and will pass away. It is demanded of every Muslim to obey the Sharia laws of Allah. The laws of the United States are man-made, while they consider Sharia law sacred, coming from the only legitimate god, Allah.

Three books make up the foundation of Sharia. There are many people who think that the Quran is the Bible of Islam. That is not true. The Bible of Islam is the Quran, the Sira and the Hadith; these three texts can be called the Trilogy. Each ruling or law in Sharia is based on a reference in the Quran or the Sunna, the perfect example of Mohammed found in two texts-Hadith and Sira. Each and every law must have its origins in the Quran and the Sunna.

In fact, the Quran is a small part–only 14% of the total words–of the doctrine that is Islam. The text devoted to the Sunna (Sira and Hadith) is 86% of the total textual doctrine of Islam. The point being Islam is 14% Allah, and 86% Mohammed!

Sharia is nothing more than a condensation and extrapolation of the Quran and the Sunna. It is impossible to understand Sharia without some understanding about the doctrine found in the Quran, Hadith and the Sira.

Please understand Islam is not just a religion, but a complete civilization with a detailed political system, religion and legal code (Sharia). There are exceptions of course, but survey after survey indicate that, when Muslims immigrate to other countries (including the United States) many have no intention of assimilating into the host country. Rather, the intent is for the host country to adapt to their form of a political, religious and legal code. I would hasten to add that many Muslims do otherwise observe our laws and traditions. But the fact remains that, in order to follow the teachings of Mohammed, a Muslim must adhere to the strict tenants of Sharia.

Here are a few examples of demands made in our society by Muslims for accommodations rooted in Sharia law:

- When schools are asked to give up a room for Islamic prayer, that is asking us to implement Sharia law.
- No course at the college level uses critical thinking regarding the history and doctrine of Islam. Under Sharia, nothing about Islam may be criticized.

• When a Muslim woman wears a headscarf, that is in obedience to Sharia law.
• When our newspapers would not publish the Danish Mohammed cartoons, our newspapers were submitting to the demands of Sharia law.
• Muslim foot-baths are being installed in airport facilities, paid for by American tax dollars. This is in accordance with Sharia law.
• We have spilled the blood of American soldiers fighting wars in Iraq and Afghanistan, only to implement a constitution whose first article is the supremacy of Sharia law.
• When our textbooks have to be vetted by Muslim organizations before they are used in our schools, that is in accordance with Sharia law.[6]

Where has Sharia Law Spread?

If you want to know how far the 'creeping cancer" of Sharia Law has spread you won't find much information from the mainstream media or government sources. There is plenty of information to be found from credible sources, you just have to look for it. I maintain that Sharia law is now a global threat, putting the very existence of liberty and democracy around the world at risk.

Many Muslims across the globe embrace Sharia Law (Islamic and Koranic law) and believe that it should be adopted as "the law of the land," according to a new report by The Pew Forum on Religion and Public Life.

"Based on more than 38,000 face-to-face interviews with Muslims in Europe, Asia, the Middle East and Africa, the survey offers in-depth research about the lives and views of Islamic adherents across the globe. Of course, there are differences among beliefs based on both region and county. But perhaps the most intriguing elements observed are the findings that many of the Muslims who want Sharia Law in a number of countries also embrace harsh penalties such as stoning for adulterers and thieves' hands being cut off. As for apostasy (those individuals who renounce Islam), there wasn't as much support among adherents surveyed. As for Muslims who believe that Sharia should be the law of the land, at least half of those surveyed in six of the 20 countries report supporting executions for apostates. Egypt (86%), Jordan (82%) and Palestine (66%) agree with this notion.

When asked whether Sharia is the revealed word of God, in 17 of the 23 nations where the question was asked, at least half of believers answered affirmatively. The proportions of those claiming that Sharia came directly from God versus those who believe that it was developed by man from God's word differ, depending on the country in which respondents were asked."[7]

If you believe we have escaped infiltration by those who wish to impose Islam's legal system in the United States of America, consider this. According to many experts, we have reached Phase 3 of the 5 phases of the spread of Islam.

Phase 1 - Arrival (Already happened)
Phase 2 - Recognition (Ongoing)
Phase 3 - Penetration (Where we are now)
Phase 4 - Confrontation (Where we are headed)
Phase 5 - Imposition (Majority of the population)[8]

However, it is also true that there are a number of court cases that involve direct conflict between civil law and Sharia law. Many American State legislatures have introduced bills banning civil/federal courts from any accommodation of Sharia. Sadly, those bills have languished and stalled because of challenges in court by Muslim groups that determined to campaign against any politician who would sponsor a bill banning any accommodation to Sharia law.

Oklahoma's law banning Sharia law from courts has been struck down. Only Louisiana, Arizona, North Carolina, South Dakota, Tennessee, Kansas and Alabama have successfully passed Sharia law-limiting legislation but only after removing the word, "Sharia."

According to a billionbible.org post, "While defending the status quo in legislatures, Sharia law has been advancing in other American institutions."[9]

- They claim the number of American public schools with Muslim students holding Islamic prayers towards Mecca is increasing. Meanwhile American public universities continue to construct Muslim-only washing facilities.
- In 2014, Rocky Mountain High School in Fort Collins, Colorado became the first high school to recite the *Pledge of Allegiance* in Arabic, replacing "One nation under God," with "One nation under Allah."
- In 1996, Bill Clinton became the first US president to hold an Eid al-Fitr dinner at the White House to celebrate the end of Ramadan, the Muslim month-long dawn-to-dusk fast. Eid al-Fitr includes six "Takbirs," the raising of hands and shouting, "Allahu Akbar!" to declare that Allah, the moon god, is the "Greatest."
- In 2000, the Republican National Convention closed the first day's proceedings with a Muslim prayer.
- In 2007, the Quran was, for the first time, used to swear into office a new US Congressman, Keith Ellison.
- In 2009, a Christian US soldier at Baghran Air Force Base in Afghanistan received Bibles in two local languages sent by his American church. The US military confiscated those Bibles for fear of retaliation if distributed and instead of at least returning them to the church, burned them.
- To attract and manage (Middle Eastern) Muslim wealth, an increasing number of American financial institutions are becoming Sharia-compliant, which requires a percentage of their annual profits be donated to Islamic organizations designated by their Sharia-compliance advisors, many of whom are members of the Muslim Brotherhood and funnel money to terrorist groups. Donations must go to one or more of eight recipient categories, one

of which is Jihad.

'No-Go Zones' May be Coming to a City Near You!

Are 'No-Go' zones a myth or a fact? This aspect of Islamic influence is polarizing and hotly debated, causing political sparks internationally.

Today, it is believed that there are certain parts of London where minority controlled communities have made it clear that local law enforcement is not welcome. It is reported that they are operating their own justice systems, according to the Chief Inspector of Constabulary, Tom Winsor. Lauren Richardson reports in a post on truthuncensored.net, "Honor killings, domestic violence, sexual abuse of children, and female genital mutilations are just some of the offenses that are believed to be unreported in some cities and growing at an alarming rate.

It starts off innocently enough with them wanting to share a neighborhood with like-minded, religious thinking community dwellers. They slowly grow larger, and incorporate more Muslims into the area, and begin buying up property as fast as it becomes available or leasing it. Then they install their own courts, government, justice and punishment system, Sharia law. At that point, threats are aimed at anyone living in the neighborhood that is non-Muslim. These areas have been formed with 'ethnic cleansing' harassment tactics; forcing existing residents out of their homes by Muslim provocation and fear of property damage and physical harm. It's very effective, and the results advantageous to the Muslim community in establishing another 'no-go' Sharia controlled zone."

Not only are 'No-Go' zones reported to be spreading across Europe, we now are being told these "do not enter" zones are popping up in American cities. Richardson claims, "They declare it by hanging signs that say: You are entering a Sharia controlled zone, Islamic rules enforced. Do not enter unless you are willing to submit to Islamic Sharia law, or risk great personal harm."[10]

"In Dearborn, Michigan, over 100,000 Muslims, 45% of the city, has settled into their first 'no-go' zone. The city and police officials have been sued in many cases that allege discrimination "against Christians" effectively by the authorities applying Sharia law. Dearborn-Dar-al-Islam, (a place governed by Islamic Sharia law). The new idea of 'no-go' and 'no-entry' is significant, and shockingly being upheld. They provide weapons and guards and government officials in their own societies. They build what they want on their compounds. They have schools inside that their kids are educated in. They are taught their religion in school.

In these areas strict Muslim ideology rules, not the rules of the host country or state they are residing in. By shutting themselves into closed communities and then demanding immunity from our criticism and our courts they become, in effect, self governing in a "voluntary apartheid." The frightening part of it all is that they are getting away with it![11]

Sharia law is demonic, and incompatible with the Constitution of the United States.

Sharia law is based primarily on principles that are contrary to our own laws, and therefore any accommodation made to this system flies in the face of our founding principles. Sharia is not a good idea. When you hear politicians and religious leaders of different faiths commend Islam as a 'religion of peace' you have to wonder if they have any idea what it really means to be a Muslim.

According to muliple books on Islam including: "Sharia Law for Non-Muslims" by Dr. Bill Warner, p.3; "It's All About Islam" by Jake Neuman, p. 138; "Killing the Quran" by Jake Neuman, p. 140 and others, under Sharia:

- There is no freedom of speech
- There is no freedom of artistic expression
- There is no freedom of religion
- There is no freedom of the press

• There is no equality between a Muslim and a non-Muslim
• Apostates can and often times face the death penalty
• There is no equal protection under different classes of people
• LGBT has no protection whatsoever, and in some countries face immediate death
• Women do not share equal rights with men
• A non-Muslim cannot bear arms
• Non-Muslims are third class citizens
• Sharia cannot be interpreted nor can it be changed to fit the existing laws

Who Are the Allies of Sharia Law?

When you look behind the veil you will see the Islamization of America is picking up steam. Sharia is not only spreading in the court system, but is also making its way into the political, educational and informational systems of our country.

According to billionbibles.org, the estimated population of Muslims in the USA is currently around five million. It is equal in size to the Hispanic population of the U.S. 27 years ago. However statistical experts tell us the Muslim population in the U.S. is growing six times faster than the national average. Much of the growth can be attributed to immigration, conversions and high birth rates among Muslims.[12]

The site states that, "Islam's growth in American prisons is particularly troubling. About 80% of Americans who convert to a religion while in prison become Muslims, who now comprise about 20% of the American prison population. The conversion rate is especially high among African-American inmates."[13]

This evil system cannot succeed on its own, it must have help. According to many credible sources, Islamic influence has infiltrated into the highest levels of our own government.

The White House now has a White House Muslim Advisor, who has counterpart Muslim advisors at the U.S. Department of

Justice, the FBI, and the U.S. Department of Homeland Security, whose Senior Fellow Mohamed Elibiary recently tweeted that America is an "Islamic country".

The website discoverthenetworks.org claims former Secretary of State Hillary Clinton's closest aide, Deputy Chief of Staff, Huma Abedin, "has three family members connected to Muslim Brotherhood operatives and/or organizations.

In December 2012, Egypt's Rose El-Youssef magazine asserted that six highly-placed Muslim Brotherhood infiltrators within the Obama administration had transformed the United States "from a position hostile to Islamic groups and organizations in the world to the largest and most important supporter of the Muslim Brotherhood."

What is the Muslim Brotherhood?

Billionbibles.org reports, "The Muslim Brotherhood Movement (Hizb al-Ikhwan al-Muslimun) or simply 'Muslim Brotherhood' or 'Ikhwan' is the oldest, largest and the best camouflaged Islamic Jihad movement in the world today and it appears to be gaining influence in the Federal Government.

To non-Muslims, the Muslim Brotherhood portrays itself as the 'acceptable branch of Islam' that promotes Muslims' socio-political integration, religious protection and economic welfare through charity, public relations and other peaceful actions. Muslims, however, know the Muslim Brotherhood as a thinly veiled Jihadist movement whose ultimate goal is to subjugate the world under Quran's Sharia law through 'Jihad.' The official motto of the Muslim Brotherhood makes this explicitly clear:

'Allah is our objective.
The Prophet is our leader.
The Quran is our law.
Jihad is our way.
Dying in the way of Allah is our highest hope.'[14]

The strategy of the Muslim Brotherhood, centered around a secret 100-year plan to subjugate the world under Islam, was to be kept hidden from people outside the organization. Authored by Sa'id Ramadan, the brother-in-law of Hassan al-Banna, the founder of Ikhwan, the plan was hidden until a police raid in Switzerland turned up a copy of The Project."

'The Project': A Manifesto of World Domination

Billionbibles.org continues, "In 1982, the Muslim Brotherhood created a manifesto titled *"The Project,"* penned by Sa'id Ramadan, the son-in-law of Hassan al-Banna, the founder of the Muslim Brotherhood. *The Project* was distributed to members around the world, who were ordered to strictly guard its content from outsiders. They did so until November of 2001, when a copy was discovered during a police raid of a senior Muslim Brotherhood financier's home in Switzerland. *The Project* outlined the Muslim Brotherhood's 25 strategies, including the deception of Taqiyya, lying to advance Islam and/or to prevent harm to Muslims, to infiltrate, and to eventually subjugate the rest of the world under Islam." (See Appendix on page 203.)

In light of what we know to be true, what can we do? Are we helpless and hopeless against the rising tide of Islamic extremists? Do we just sit back and allow those who are killing in the name of their religion to continue, while at the same time admitting more adherents to the same ideology into this country?

Are we going to adopt the same naïve, simplistic and dangerous ideology of British Prime Minister Neville Chamberlain? He became known as the 'apostle of appeasement' as he and the leaders of France did everything possible to appease Adolf Hitler. They built their sand castles of appeasement on the hope that Hitler would not plunge Europe into another World War. Their naïveté was expressed in their desire to heal the wounds of the first World War and to correct what many believed were injustices done to Germany at the *Treaty of Versailles.* It was Chamberlain who is famously quoted saying, "We should seek by all means in our power to avoid war, by analyzing possible causes, by trying to remove them, by discussion in a spirit of collaboration and good will."[15] They were mistaken in trying to appease Hitler, and millions of lives were lost in the horror of World War II. It was Winston Churchill who recognized the danger of appeasement, He said, "An appeaser is one who feeds a crocodile, hoping it will eat him last."[16]

It is time for Christians to find their voice and understand that we do not *"wrestle against flesh and blood, but against principalities, against powers, against the rulers of the darkness of this age, against spiritual hosts of wickedness in the heavenly places" (Ephesians 6:12).*

We must put on the whole armor of God, (Ephesians 6:11-18), and use *"the sword of the Spirit, which is the word of God"* to witness to Muslims. The gospel of Jesus Christ is the only power that can break through the darkness of sin, and the deception of the antichrist spirit.

Are you willing to acknowledge the fact that Islam and Christianity will not and cannot ever be reconciled as one faith? Although Islam recognizes Jesus as a prophet, it does not recognize the atoning death, burial and resurrection of Christ. It fervently rejects the deity of Christ, and contends that Mohammed is the only way to find truth. As long as we keep silent, Islam will advance across the globe. But know this . . . all of the darkness in the world cannot put out the light that shines when the Gospel of Jesus Christ is burning brightly in truth. When the body of Christ is strong, Islam has no place to penetrate. But when the body of Christ is weak and sits silently in the pews, ascribing to a powerless form of Christianity, Islam will continue to penetrate and fill the void. Who is in control? Who is pulling the strings?

Heed the words of the apostle Paul as translated in The Message:

"The world is unprincipled. It's dog-eat-dog out there! The world doesn't fight fair. But we don't live or fight our battles that way—never have and never will. The tools of our trade aren't for marketing or manipulation, but they are for demolishing that entire massively corrupt culture. We use our powerful God-tools for smashing warped philosophies, tearing down barriers erected against the truth of God, fitting every loose thought and emotion and impulse into the structure of life shaped by Christ. Our tools are ready at hand for clearing the ground of every obstruction and building lives of obedience into maturity."
2 Corinthians 10:3-6 MSG

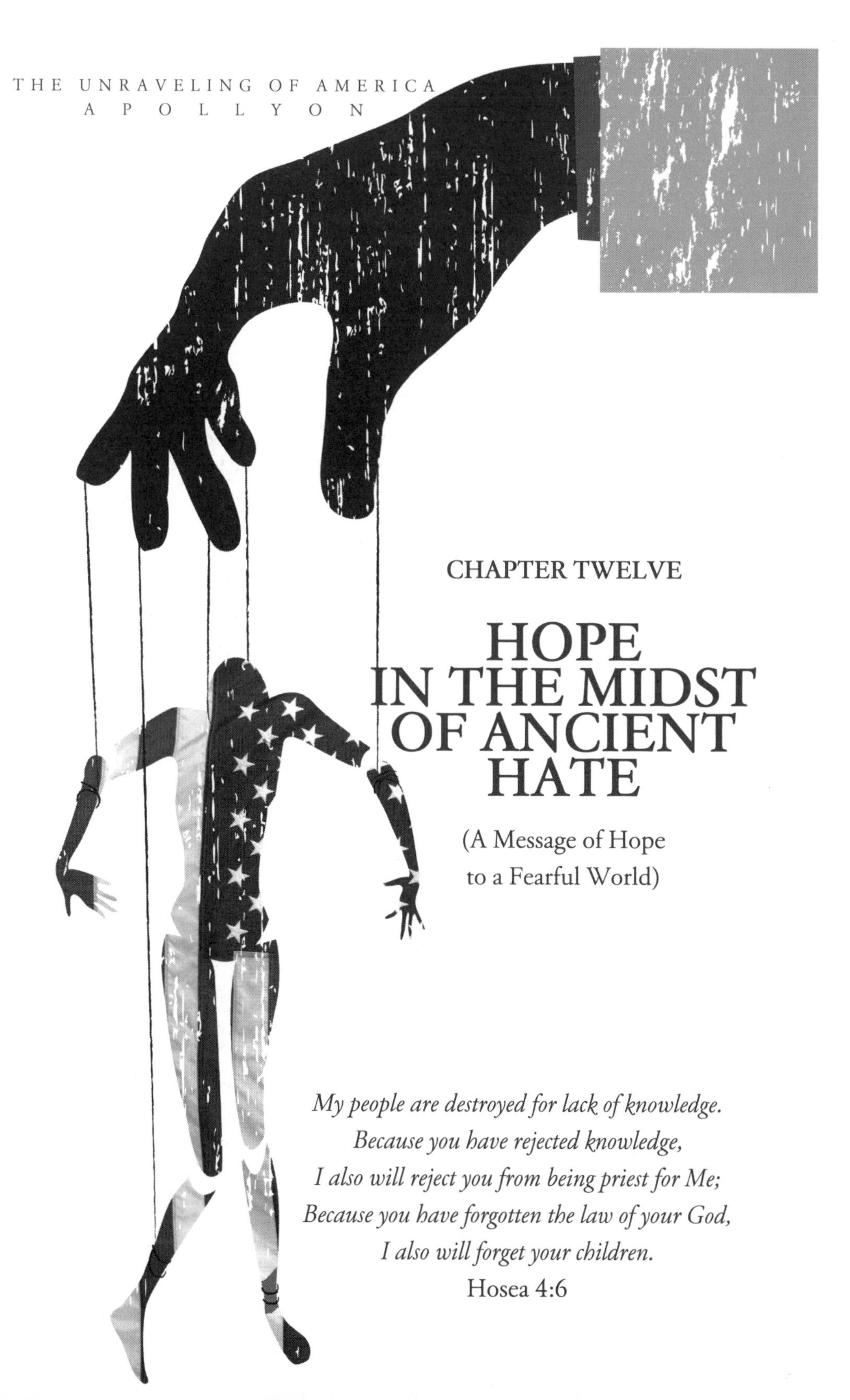

CHAPTER TWELVE

HOPE IN THE MIDST OF ANCIENT HATE

(A Message of Hope to a Fearful World)

My people are destroyed for lack of knowledge.
Because you have rejected knowledge,
I also will reject you from being priest for Me;
Because you have forgotten the law of your God,
I also will forget your children.
Hosea 4:6

"Darkness cannot drive out darkness: only light can do that.
Hate cannot drive out hate: only love can do that."
Martin Luther King Jr.[1]

Several months ago the Lord began to show me prophetic insight about current events taking place in the world. In my lifetime, I have never seen as much hatred and viciousness as I am seeing today. In these final pages, I will trace the source of a hate that transcends time and breaches national borders. The divisions and social upheaval we face today are rooted in the past, not the present.

Again, my goal in writing this book is to compile truth and give you knowledge about the true condition of our world, and what is at stake if we are not informed and engaged in our culture. The Lord took me to the first part of Hosea 4:6: *"My people are destroyed for lack of knowledge."* He showed me a lack of knowledge will always lead to confusion. A faulty view of past history and current circumstances will open the door to deception.

In Hosea 4:6 The Lord did not say:

- My people are destroyed for lack of Church attendance.
- My people are destroyed for lack of spiritual gifts.
- My people are destroyed for the lack of money.
- My people are destroyed for lack of worship.

NO - He said it was a lack of knowledge!

In chapter two, I exposed the spirit of Apollyon, which is nothing more than the "spirit of deception." That spirit is threatening to overtake this country in a spectacular fashion. My desire is not to be offensive to anyone, but there has come a time when we admit something very strange is happening in America. We must look around and ask ourselves, "Have we lost our collective minds?" It was that great philosopher, Forrest Gump, who said it best: "Stupid is as stupid does."

Our ignorance knows no bounds. Dumb is not the result of a poor education (or no), but a "blindness" to the truth. This mindlessness is not isolated to any one political party or segment of society. It is a spirit that will affect anyone of any political persuasion, conservative and liberal alike.

Hate Speech in Education

We are facing a serious threat creeping across college campuses and universities. Some have called it the only "hate speech" allowed in campus 'safe places.' And, what is that? "Anti-Semitism!"

Lawrence H Summers, Charles W. Eliot University Professor at Harvard University said in a Washington Post article, "It has seemed to me that a vast double standard regarding what constitutes prejudice exists on American college campuses. There is hypersensitivity to prejudice against most minority groups but what might be called hyper-insensitivity to anti-Semitism."[2]

Summers sites numerous examples of hyper-sensitivity to actions of university students.

- At Bowdoin College, holding parties with sombreros and tequila is deemed to be an act of prejudice against Mexicans.
- At Emory University, the chalking of an endorsement of the likely 2016 Republican presidential candidate, Donald Trump, on a sidewalk is deemed to require a review of security tapes.
- The existence of a college named after a widely admired former US president has been condemned at Princeton, under the duress of a student occupation.
- At Yale, Halloween costumes are the subject of administrative edict.
- The dean of Harvard Law School has acknowledged that

hers is a racist institution, while the freshman dean at Harvard College has used dinner place mats to propagandize the student body on aspects of diversity.

• Professors acquiesce as students insist that they not be exposed to views on issues, such as abortion, that make them uncomfortable.

Summers contends that this is, "Inconsistent with the basic American values of free speech and open debate. It fails to recognize that a proper liberal education should cause moments of acute discomfort as cherished beliefs are challenged."

He goes on to report:

• Nearly a dozen academic associations have enacted formal boycotts of Israeli institutions, and in some cases, Israeli scholars.

• Student governments at dozens of universities have demanded the divestiture of companies that do business in Israel or the West Bank.

• Guest speakers, and even some faculty in their classrooms, compare Israel to Nazi Germany and question its right to continued existence as a Jewish State.

"Yet, with very few exceptions, university leaders who are so quick to stand up against micro-aggressions against other groups remain silent in the face of anti-Semitism. Indeed, many major American universities, including Harvard, remain institutional members of associations that are engaged in boycotts of Israel. The idea of divesting Israel is opposed only in the same way that divesting apartheid South Africa was opposed — as an inappropriate intrusion into politics, not as immoral or anti-Semitic."[3]

Hate is not just directed toward the Jewish people. Christians are also increasingly targets of the same insidious spirit seeking to destroy any signs of the true and living God.

Where does all this hate and confusion come from? In order to understand what is happening now, and what will take place in the future, you have to go back to ancient prophecy found in the book of Ezekiel. It is up to this generation of believers to expose and break the cycle of hate. It will not come through protest marches or new laws. It will only come when the Church regains her voice and begins to speak with authority to the nations of the world.

The Lord showed me that there is an ancient prophecy and a promise given to those who have eyes to see and hearts to believe. He challenged me to "ponder" these ancient prophecies and promises and then I would have an understanding of the signs of times.

> *I cried out to God with my voice—To God with my voice; And He gave ear to me. In the day of my trouble I sought the Lord; My hand was stretched out in the night without ceasing; My soul refused to be comforted. I remembered God, and was troubled; I complained, and my spirit was overwhelmed. Selah you hold my eyelids open; I am so troubled that I cannot speak. I have considered the days of old, The years of ancient times.*
> Psalm 77:1-5

> *Tell and bring forth your case; yes, let them take counsel together. Who has declared this from ancient time? Who has told it from that time? Have not I, the Lord? And there is no other God besides Me, a just God and a Savior; There is none besides Me.*
> Isaiah 45:21

> *Declaring the end from the beginning, and from ancient times things that are not yet done, saying, 'My counsel shall stand, and I will do all My pleasure . . .*
> Isaiah 46:10

The word "ancient" is the key word. It comes from a Hebrew word "Olam," which has several distinct meanings:

- From everlasting to everlasting
- Beyond time

- Eternity
- The world without end
- That which is veiled as a secret
- And, that which has a beginning before creation and beyond this dimension.

Next, the Lord took me to Ezekiel 35-37 and pointed out how this portion of Scripture unfolds shockingly clear prophecies about last days judgment and strategic alignments on the earth. He told me if I would study these ancient prophecies, I would have a clear picture of what we are going through right now, and with it, a promised hope for the future. I saw three things.

THE ANCIENT HATRED

> *Moreover the word of the Lord came to me, saying, "Son of man, set your face against Mount Seir and prophesy against it, and say to it, 'Thus says the Lord God: "Behold, O Mount Seir, I am against you; I will stretch out My hand against you, and make you most desolate; I shall lay your cities waste, and you shall be desolate. Then you shall know that I am the Lord. "Because you have had an ancient hatred, and have shed the blood of the children of Israel by the power of the sword at the time of their calamity, when their iniquity came to an end,"*
> Ezekiel 35:1-5

Here is the word "ancient" regarding Middle Eastern issues. Ezekiel 35 is a warning to the nations around Israel. He specifically points to the nations in the shadow of "Mount Seir," which would include Saudi Arabia, Egypt, Southern Jordan, all of North Africa, and Yemen. The desire of those nations was to take over two nations.

The ancient hatred did not just begin with Ezekiel's prophecy - it goes all the way back to the beginning.

War was declared in the Garden of Eden!

> *And I will put enmity (Hatred)*
> *Between you and the woman,*
> *And between your seed and her Seed;*
> *He shall bruise your head,*
> *And you shall bruise His heel."*
> Genesis 3:15

Do you see the word "enmity?" It is the same word as "hatred" found in Ezekiel 35:5. Hate is one of the strongest words in the human vocabulary. What is all this hatred about? Where did it start? To find the source you have to go all the way back to the beginning of life on the earth. Humans are not supposed to hate each other, but tragically an ancient hatred has been festering since the Garden of Eden.

God declared that there would be a hatred between His seed and the seed of the enemy! Many people think what is going on in the Middle East today is something new. It's not. For the most part, people have little knowledge of history. They have no understanding of the Balfour Declaration, the restoration of Israel, and know nothing about Winston Churchill drawing national borders in the Middle East. And, since a realistic view of history is not being taught on college campuses, we should not wonder why many college students are anti-Semitic and anti-American.

I want you to understand that the hatred planted in the hearts and minds of people is the spirit of Apollyon, the destroyer. It uses the spirit of deception that blinds men to the truth. If you look at this worldwide hatred directed towards the nation of Israel with an objective and discerning eye you see it makes no sense whatsoever.

The word *enmity* also means to hate someone of another racial identity. It is the ancient word for racism. Original racism was anti-semitism. Sadly, many races have a combined hatred for the people of Israel, and what they don't understand is they are taking the side of the original racist, Satan himself!

Today, extreme Islamists see other humans as objects of hatred and wrath. This ancient hatred was rooted in the heart of Satan, appeared in the Garden of Eden and continues today! All hatred, all racial division, and all hate for the nation of Israel is rooted in the ancient enmity that declared war on the human race in the Garden of Eden.

You have to know that God has not forgotten, even in the face of what looks like a defeat for the people of God. It may look like ISIS is winning, and racial Islam is marching to take over the world. It may look like the forces of political correctness are overwhelming America. But, the final chapter has not been written. God has not forgotten His promises to Israel, the apple of His eye. He is not oblivious to the ancient hatred.

When you begin to track that ancient hatred, you can see it woven throughout Scripture and human history.

- Pharaoh ordered the killing of the firstborn of Israel. (Exodus 1:1-22).
- The captivity and overthrow of Israel by Babylon and Nebuchadnezzar in 722BC and 586BC.
- Antiochus Epiphanes devastated Jerusalem in 168BC. He defiled the Temple, offered a pig on its altar, erected an altar to Jupiter, prohibited Temple worship, forbade circumcision on pain of death, and sold thousands of Jewish families into slavery.
- In 70AD, Titus completely destroyed Jerusalem and sacked the Temple, killing thousands of Jews.
- In the 20th century, Adolf Hitler was responsible for killing over 6 million Jews, not including other minority groups.
- In the gulags of Russia, Joseph Stalin was responsible for killing more Jews than Hitler.

Christians have also been the target of tribal and racial hatred.

- On April 24, 1915, the systematic slaughter of over 1.5 million Armenian Christians by Muslims began.
- Today, the brutal persecution of religious minorities is continuing under the boot of an ever-increasing Islamic government in Turkey. Until the Muslims took control, Turkey was 95% Christian. Today, religious minorities (non-Muslims) are being eliminated, and yet the West remains silent.
- ISIS is continually waging "holy war" to this very hour, and you and I both know that if our current administration had the heart and will, ISIS could be eliminated in 3 days!
- Mostly ignored by the mainstream media was the threat by ISIS to crucify a Catholic priest on Good Friday. Father Tom Uzhunnalil was kidnapped by ISIS gunmen in Yemen, killing at least 15 innocent people. The terrorists carried out their threat and crucified Father Uzhunnalil, according to the Archbishop of Vienna, Cardinal Christoph Schönborn.
- Over one hundred years ago, Sir Winston Churchill saw the impending threat posed by Islam. He said, "No stronger retrograde force exists in the world. Far from being moribund, Mohammedanism is a militant and proselytizing faith. It has already spread throughout Central Africa, raising fearless warriors at every step; and were it not that Christianity is sheltered in the strong arms of science, the science against which it had vainly struggled, the civilization of modern Europe might fall, as fell the civilization of ancient Rome."[4]

In our own country, you can see racial hatred is coming to a boiling point. While we're being told we are a racist nation, this so-called racist nation elected an African-American president, not once, but twice. Currently, Mr. Obama has been in office for nearly 8 years, and in my lifetime, I have never seen the racial strife and divisions like we are seeing today - and that is saying something!

My wife and I have fought racism our entire ministry. We stood with Dr. Martin Luther King Jr. in Montgomery, and in every church I pastored, we fostered an openness to all races. We hold the same belief as Dr. King–All lives matter!

What began in Eden is being fostered by the demonic spirit of Apollyon. This demonic spirit will use anything and anyone to pull the strings of society and advance the agenda of hate! What the enemy did not count on or understand was that Yahweh was there, watching all of these deeds of hate and He will bring judgment.

> *"Because you have said, 'These two nations and these two countries shall be mine, and we will possess them,' although the Lord was there, therefore, as I live," says the Lord God, "I will do according to your anger and according to the envy which you showed in your hatred against them; and I will make Myself known among them when I judge you. Then you shall know that I am the Lord. I have heard all your blasphemies which you have spoken against the mountains of Israel, saying, 'They are desolate; they are given to us to consume.'"*
> Ezekiel 35:10-12

Who are these two "end-time" nations? I have come to the conclusion these two nations are Israel and the United States of America. This ancient hatred has two desires, to possess Israel and to destroy the United States. But, I want you to know that no matter how hard the enemy tries, he will ultimately fail because God declared in Ezekiel 35:11, *"I will do according to your anger and according to the envy which you showed in your hatred against them; and I will make Myself known among them when I judge you. Then you shall know that I am the Lord."*

THE ANCIENT HEIGHTS

Moving further into the book of Ezekiel, the Lord showed me a second thing, the ancient heights.

"And you, son of man, prophesy to the mountains of Israel, and say, 'O mountains of Israel, hear the word of the Lord! Thus says the Lord God: "Because the enemy has said of you, 'Aha! The ancient heights have become our possession,'"' therefore prophesy, and say, 'Thus says the Lord God: "Because they made you desolate and swallowed you up on every side, so that you became the possession of the rest of the nations, and you are taken up by the lips of talkers and slandered by the people"— therefore, O mountains of Israel, hear the word of the Lord God! Thus says the Lord God to the mountains, the hills, the rivers, the valleys, the desolate wastes, and the cities that have been forsaken, which became plunder and mockery to the rest of the nations all around— therefore thus says the Lord God: "Surely I have spoken in My burning jealousy against the rest of the nations and against all Edom, who gave My land to themselves as a possession, with wholehearted joy and spiteful minds, in order to plunder its open country."'

"Therefore prophesy concerning the land of Israel, and say to the mountains, the hills, the rivers, and the valleys, 'Thus says the Lord God: "Behold, I have spoken in My jealousy and My fury, because you have borne the shame of the nations." Therefore thus says the Lord God: "I have raised My hand in an oath that surely the nations that are around you shall bear their own shame.
Ezekiel 36:1-7

Notice in verse two the mention of the "ancient heights." Remember I already showed you the word translated "ancient" in the Hebrew is "Olam" and one of its meanings is "everlasting." There is a desire to possess the mountains of Israel, especially the "Temple Mount." Why are the mountains of Israel called "ancient?" What is it about these mountains, stretching from "vanishing point to vanishing point," that is so controversial and coveted? To understand that, we have to go where it all started.

Back to the Beginning

I believe scripture shows us that we are sitting on a rebuilt earth. Between Genesis 1:1 and 1:2 something happened. *"In the beginning God created the heavens and the earth. The earth was without form, and void;"* (Genesis 1:1-2). The word means it "became" formless, a wasteland, like a desert. Whatever was there before is there no more. Between Genesis 1:1 and 1:2, there is a time gap. God created the earth in verse 1. In verse 2, it became a wasteland.

There was a prior earth inhabited by animals and a race of beings that we know nothing about. There was an earth here before there was an earth as described in the creation story (Isaiah 45:18; 2 Peter 3:5-6). I repeat, something happened between Genesis 1:1 and Genesis 1:2.

This idea of a prior earth is also found in Jeremiah 4: 23-26, *"I beheld the earth, and indeed it was without form, and void; And the heavens, they had no light. I beheld the mountains, and indeed they trembled, And all the hills moved back and forth. I beheld, and indeed there was no man, And all the birds of the heavens had fled. I beheld, and indeed the fruitful land was a wilderness, And all its cities were broken down at the presence of the Lord, by His fierce anger."*

What Jeremiah shows us is that the world was not created in vain. There was an ancient world teeming with life, but something catastrophic happened that destroyed the original Earth.

What do we know about that original earth in relationship to the "ancient heights?" The Bible tells us that there was a cherubim named Lucifer who had been given the assignment to rule over that ancient earth.

The record of Lucifer's rule is also found in Ezekiel:

1. He is a created being (Ezekiel 28:13).
2. He was perfect, but chose to rebel (Ezekiel 28:15).
3. He was beautiful (Ezekiel 28:12).
4. His anointing and assignment was the old earth (Ezekiel 28:13-14).

5. He lived on the "Holy Mountain of God" (Jerusalem) (Ezekiel 28:14).

From that mountain, worship went out worldwide, but Lucifer's fall destroyed the old earth and it became "without form and void!" Isaiah described Lucifer's fall in chapter 14:13-14, *"For you have said in your heart: 'I will ascend into heaven, I will exalt my throne above the stars of God; I will also sit on the mount of the congregation on the farthest sides of the north; I will ascend above the heights of the clouds, I will be like the Most High.'"*

The same one who perpetrated the "ancient hate" is the same one who believes he has ownership of the "ancient heights!" You see the "ancient heights" represent the place God rules, loves and speaks to his people (Proverbs 23:10). It was through the Jews we received the law, the ancient rites of the tabernacle, the temple, and the Ark of the Covenant.

That is why Satan has fought so furiously from the very beginning to rule from the Mountain of God! It is still going on today. Sitting on the Mountain of God, in Jerusalem, is the Dome of the Rock (a shrine), and beside it stands a mosque where Muslims pray to Allah.

That small geographic location we call Israel stretches from eternity to eternity. That little strip of land represents less than 1% of the land mass in the Middle East, yet it is the most sought-after real estate in the world. I have heard people say, "What is the big deal, and why is that little piece of land so important? Simply put – God loves it and has declared, "That's my mountain, and you can't have it!"

Satan's desire is to thwart God's people, Jew and Gentile alike, and to cut off God's life-giving revelation (Ephesians 2:4-6). Satan's desire is the "ancient heights" of Israel geographically, and the "ancient heights" of God's spiritual gateway to His people. The devil will attack any individual, church or voice that dares to live in the "high places" with the Almighty!

Habakkuk declared, after hearing the prophetic word, that *"the Lord God is my strength; He will make my feet like deer's feet, and he will make me walk on my high hills"* (Habakkuk 3:19). That promise is mine as well, according to Paul's revelation in Ephesians 2:4-6. Because of the finished work of Jesus Christ on the cross, I can also declare the "ancient heights" are mine, and Satan can't have them! Hallelujah!

THE ANCIENT HOPE

The third thing The Lord showed me is that we have an ancient and enduring hope!

> *"And who can proclaim as I do? Then let him declare it and set it in order for Me, Since I appointed the ancient people. And the things that are coming and shall come, Let them show these to them."*
> Isaiah 44:7

We need to stop worrying about what the world is coming to and rejoice over who is coming back to this world!

The ancient hope for the whole world, then and now, rests in Israel. This nation was thrice dead, but now Israel is the only dead nation to ever come back alive. It has the only dead language (Hebrew) that has come back alive. It has the only dead currency that is back in circulation. I would call that a miracle, wouldn't you?

In Ezekiel 35 we saw the Ancient Hate; in Ezekiel 36, the Ancient Heights; and now we come to Ezekiel 37, and we see the Ancient Hope.

> *"The hand of the Lord came upon me and brought me out in the Spirit of the Lord, and set me down in the midst of the valley; and it was full of bones. Then He caused me to pass by them all around, and behold, there were very many in the open valley; and indeed they were very dry. And He said to me, "Son of man, can these bones*

live?" So I answered, "O Lord God, You know."
Ezekiel 37:1-3

2,500 years ago, Ezekiel saw a prophetic picture. He was caught up in a vision, and I believe he saw the Holocaust, represented by a valley full of bones. His nation was already gone by then, so it wasn't about the time in which he was living, but the future according to Ezekiel 38-39.

God looked at Ezekiel and said, *"Son of man, can these bones live?"* The prophet answered Him, *"O Lord God, You know."* I love this picture. Preachers like to take this passage and preach on revival and that's fine, but this prophecy was directed toward the rebirth of Israel, not the Church.

Also He said to me, "Prophesy to the breath, prophesy, son of man, and say to the breath, 'Thus says the Lord God: "Come from the four winds, O breath, and breathe on these slain, that they may live." So I prophesied as He commanded me, and breath came into them, and they lived, and stood upon their feet, an exceedingly great army.

Then He said to me, "Son of man, these bones are the whole house of Israel. They indeed say, 'Our bones are dry, our hope is lost, and we ourselves are cut off!' Therefore prophesy and say to them, 'Thus says the Lord God: "Behold, O My people, I will open your graves and cause you to come up from your graves, and bring you into the land of Israel. Then you shall know that I am the Lord, when I have opened your graves, O My people, and brought you up from your graves. I will put My Spirit in you, and you shall live, and I will place you in your own land. Then you shall know that I, the Lord, have spoken it and performed it," says the Lord.'"
Ezekiel 37:9-14

The Lord gave him a strange command, "preach to those bones" (Ezekiel 37:4). You see, the prophetic word can cause dead bones to come alive. The wind of the Holy Spirit that blew in Genesis 1 is the same wind that blew across that valley of death. It's the same "rushing mighty wind" that blew on the day of Pentecost. It's the same "breath of God" that still causes dead men to come alive today!

The Jews are back in their land because the Lord told the prophet Ezekiel to prophesy to a valley full of death. Yes, the bones live and are back in their land for the third time! This event has stirred the whole earth. On May 15, 1948, the nation of Israel was born in a day. And since that day, there has been a "noise" resounding around the world. Today, the whole earth is focused on that tiny parcel of land!

A WORD OF HOPE IN THE MIDST OF HATE

You may be thinking, 'That's all well and good for Israel, but what about those of us who are believers?" They can't go without us, and you need to know that along with the hope for Israel is a veiled prophecy for those of us known as the Church.

Why Is David Here?

Guess who shows up in Ezekiel 37:24? *"David My servant shall be king over them."* This is a restored Israel, so what is David doing here? Not only here, but what is he doing in the book of Revelation, *"And to the angel of the church in Philadelphia write, 'These things says He who is holy, He who is true, "He who has the key of David, He who opens and no one shuts, and shuts and no one opens": (Revelation 3:7)* And, at the end of John's Revelation, after all that has taken place on the earth, He says, *"I, Jesus, have sent My angel to testify to you these things in the churches. I am the Root and the Offspring of David, the Bright and Morning Star" (Revelation 22:16).*

I have been preaching the Tabernacle of David since 1989. I have been declaring that Christians are found in prophecy along with Israel. There is a church of Jew and Gentile–a "one new man" church–that bears witness to the Jews and to the nation.

On Mount Zion, David had a Tabernacle for 33 years, representing the life of Jesus. The Zadok priesthood had a choir and orchestra that released worship 24 hours a day, 7 days a week, for 33 years. The Ark of the Covenant sat in the tent without a veil to cover it. David wrote many of the "songs of the Lord" sitting under the "wings of the Ark." Worship was open and available to all who wanted to come hear.

David's Tabernacle is very much alive today! The prophet Amos predicted that God would restore again the Tabernacle of David so that all the Gentiles might seek after the Lord (Amos 9:11-12). In the earliest days of the Christian Church, James, the brother of Jesus, repeated the words of the prophet Amos to explain that the Church, which was almost entirely Jewish, must accept Gentile converts (Acts 15:16-17). Davidic worship of praise, dancing, and Biblical music is being restored to the Church worldwide.

Did Ezekiel know any of this? He declared that alongside a reborn Israel will be the Tabernacle of David - "the one new man Church!"

"David My servant shall be king over them, and they shall all have one shepherd; they shall also walk in My judgments and observe My statutes, and do them. Then they shall dwell in the land that I have given to Jacob My servant, where your fathers dwelt; and they shall dwell there, they, their children, and their children's children, forever; and My servant David shall be their prince forever. Moreover I will make a covenant of peace with them, and it shall be an everlasting covenant with them; I will establish them and multiply them, and I will set My sanctuary in their midst forevermore. My tabernacle also shall be with them; indeed I will be their God, and they shall

be My people. The nations also will know that I, the Lord, sanctify Israel, when My sanctuary is in their midst forevermore.'"
Ezekiel 37:24-28

In these last days Israel will be in their land, and the "One New Man Church" will function as the Tabernacle of David.

Hebrews 12 records a beautiful prophecy of what end time worship should look like under an open heaven. Notice, not only Israel, but the church is called Mount Zion.

"But you have come to Mount Zion and to the city of the living God, the heavenly Jerusalem, to an innumerable company of angels, to the general assembly and church of the firstborn who are registered in heaven, to God the Judge of all, to the spirits of just men made perfect, to Jesus the Mediator of the new covenant, and to the blood of sprinkling that speaks better things than that of Abel."
Hebrews 12:22-24

It Is Time For Us to Rise to our Purpose!

- We must be bold and not give up (Ephesians 3:11-13).
- We must get on our knees and focus on the task (Ephesians 3:14-15).
- We must respond to others in love, trusting in His strength for every weakness. His church must operate with power from on High, and will see miracles released until Christ's return. (Ephesians 3:16-21)

Though ancient hatred continues to burn in the Middle East, the Word of God reveals an ancient hope, rooted firmly in the blood of Jesus, that no demon in hell can uproot. I have a hope that will endure.

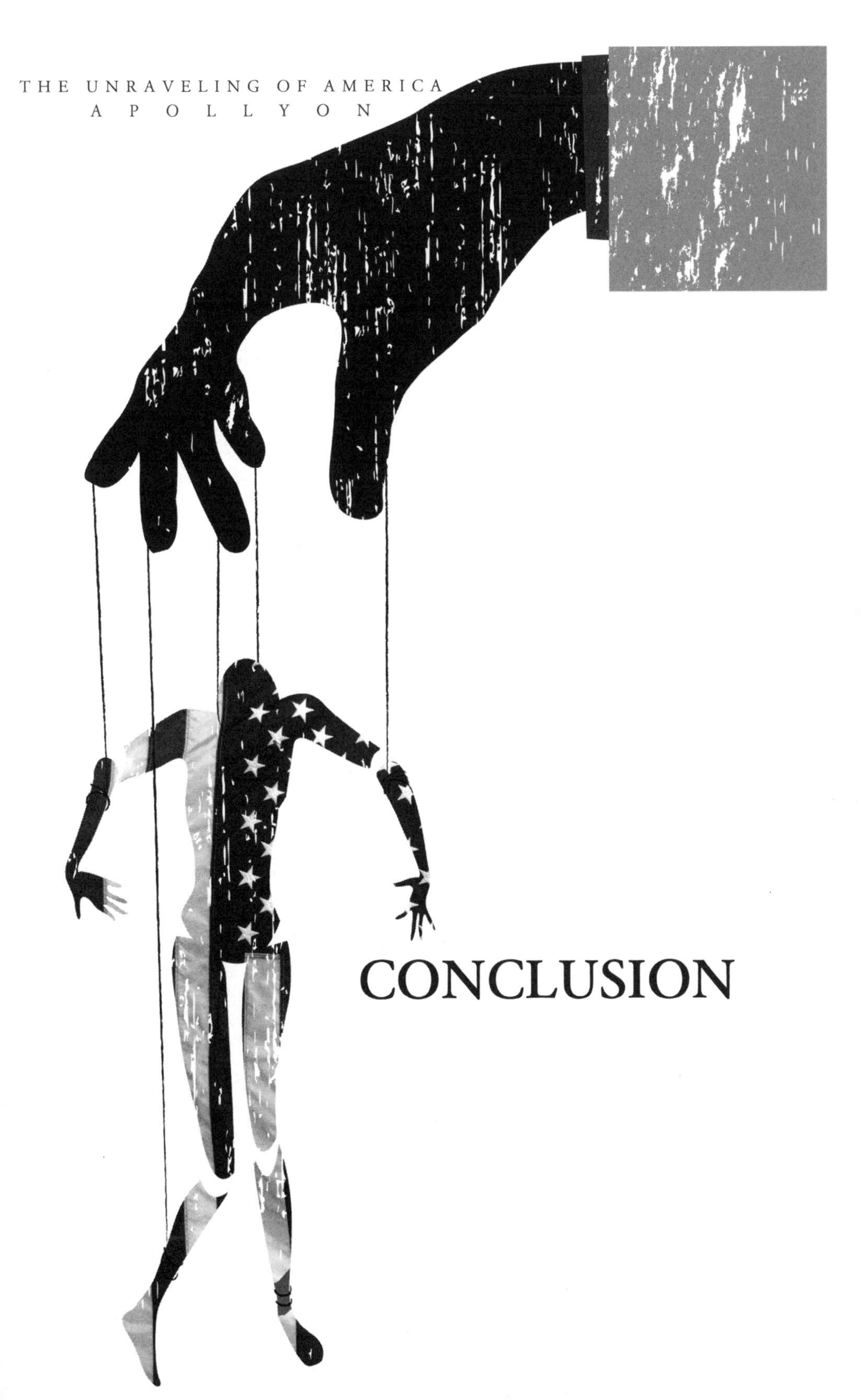

CONCLUSION

Though the forces of culture arrayed against the church and our Lord Jesus Christ seem to be overwhelming, we have hope! Jesus said in John 8:32 that only the truth can set us free. In the preceding pages, we have attempted to shed light upon important issues so that the reader can have a clear understanding of the truth. I do not believe these issues have been given a fair hearing in our media, culture, and educational system. In fact, by some, it is considered politically incorrect to even discuss them.

The Bible asks this question, "If the foundations be destroyed, what will the righteous do?" This book is an effort to tell the truth and thereby, undergird the foundations of our nation so that the generations to come can enjoy the fruits of a free society. This work is by no means exhaustive, and I have made every effort to present the truth to you with accuracy. Much needs to be done to restore Jesus Christ and the Judeo Christian values of our Founders to American culture.

When you come to the end of the movie, "The Help," which exposes racial prejudice in the South during the 1950s, Aibileen is fired by her racist boss, losing her job as a maid. She says with poignant accuracy that the solution for their problems can begin by telling the truth. There is no instant fix for America, but let's begin speaking the truth.

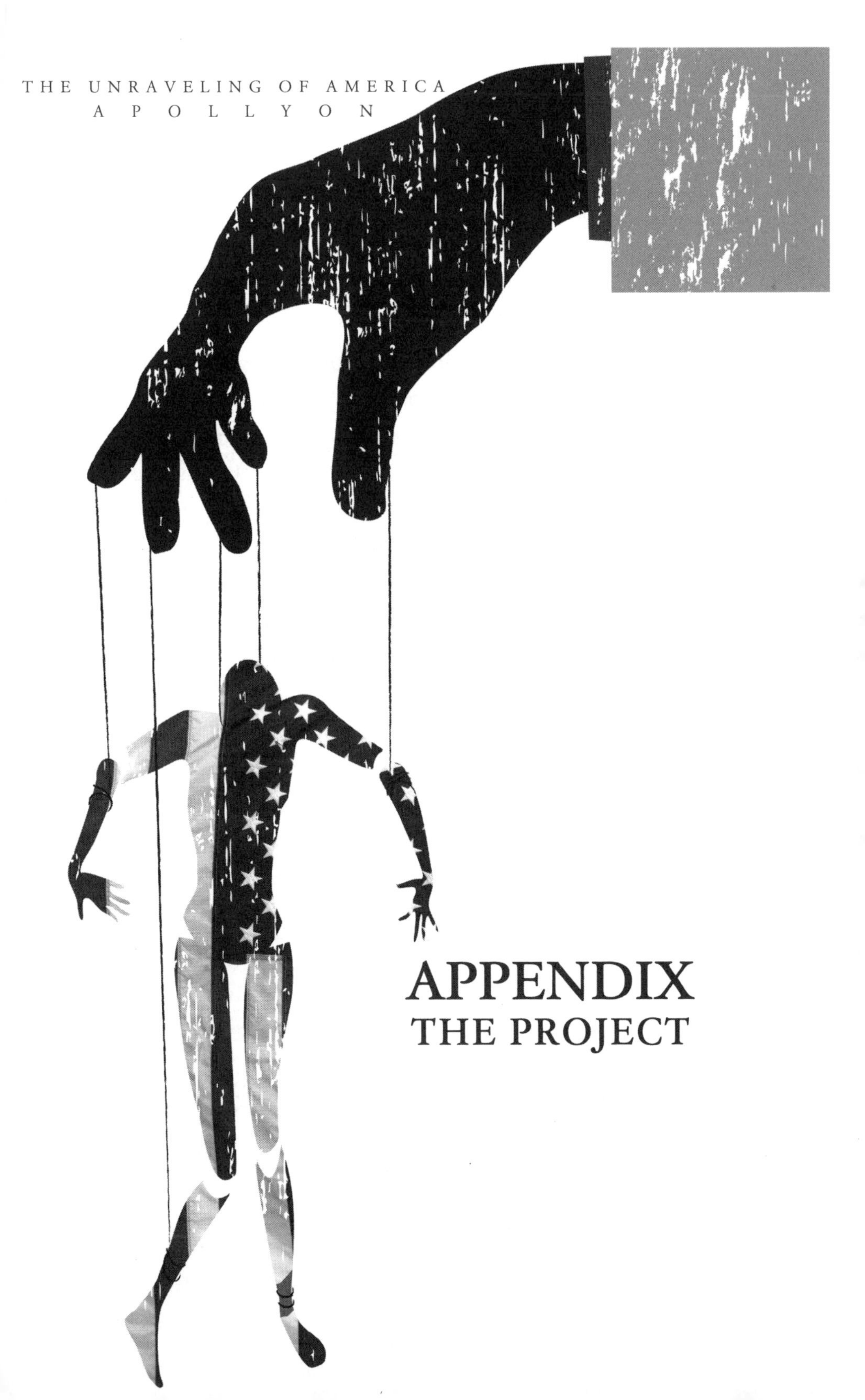

APPENDIX
THE PROJECT

'The Project': A Manifesto of World Domination

Billionbibles.org continues, "In 1982, the Muslim Brotherhood created a manifesto titled *"The Project,"* penned by Sa'id Ramadan, the son-in-law of Hassan al-Banna, the founder of the Muslim Brotherhood. *The Project* was distributed to members around the world, who were ordered to strictly guard its content from outsiders. They did so until November of 2001, when a copy was discovered during a police raid of a senior Muslim Brotherhood financier's home in Switzerland. *The Project* outlined the Muslim Brotherhood's 25 strategies, including the deception of Taqiyya, lying to advance Islam and/or to prevent harm to Muslims, to infiltrate, and to eventually subjugate the rest of the world under Islam."

1. Network and coordinate actions between like-minded Islamists organizations;
2. Avoid open alliances with known terrorist organizations and individuals to maintain the appearance of "moderation";
3. Infiltrate and take over existing Muslim organizations to realign them towards the Muslim Brotherhood's collective goals;
4. Use deception to mask the intended goals of Islamist actions, as long as it doesn't conflict with Sharia law;
5. Avoid social conflicts with Westerners locally, nationally or globally, that might damage the long-term ability to expand the Islamist power-base in the West, including the support of full-time administrators and workers;
6. Conduct surveillance, obtain data, and establish collection and data storage capabilities;
7. Put into place a watchdog system for monitoring Western media to warn Muslims of international plots fomented against them;

8. Cultivate an Islamist intellectual community, including the establishment of think-tanks and advocacy groups, and publishing "academic" studies," to legitimize Islamist positions and to chronicle the history of Islamist movements;
9. Develop a comprehensive 100-year plan to advance Islamist ideology throughout the world;
10. Balance international objectives with local flexibility;
11. Build extensive social networks of schools, hospitals and charitable organizations dedicated to Islamist ideals so that contact with the movement for Muslims in the West is constant;
12. Involve ideologically committed Muslims in democratically-elected institutions on all levels in the West, including government, NGOs, private organizations and labor unions;
13. Instrumentally use existing Western institutions until they can be converted and put into service of Islam;
14. Draft Islamic constitutions, laws and policies for eventual implementation;
15. Avoid conflict within the Islamist movements on all levels, including the development of processes for conflict resolution;
16. Institute alliances with Western "progressive" organizations that share similar goals;
17. Create autonomous "security forces" to protect Muslims in the West;
18. Inflame violence and keep Muslims living in the West "in a Jihad frame of mind";
19. Support Jihad movements across the Muslim world through preaching, propaganda, personnel, funding, and technical and operational support;
20. Make the Palestinian Issue a global wedge cause for Muslims;
21. Adopt the total liberation of Palestine from Israel and the creation of an Islamic state as a keystone in the plan for global Islamic domination;

22. Instigate a constant campaign to incite hatred by Muslims against Jews and reject any discussions of conciliation or coexistence with them;
23. Actively create Jihad terror cells within Palestine;
24. Link the terrorist activities in Palestine with the global terror movement;
25. Collect sufficient funds to indefinitely perpetuate and support Jihad around the world.

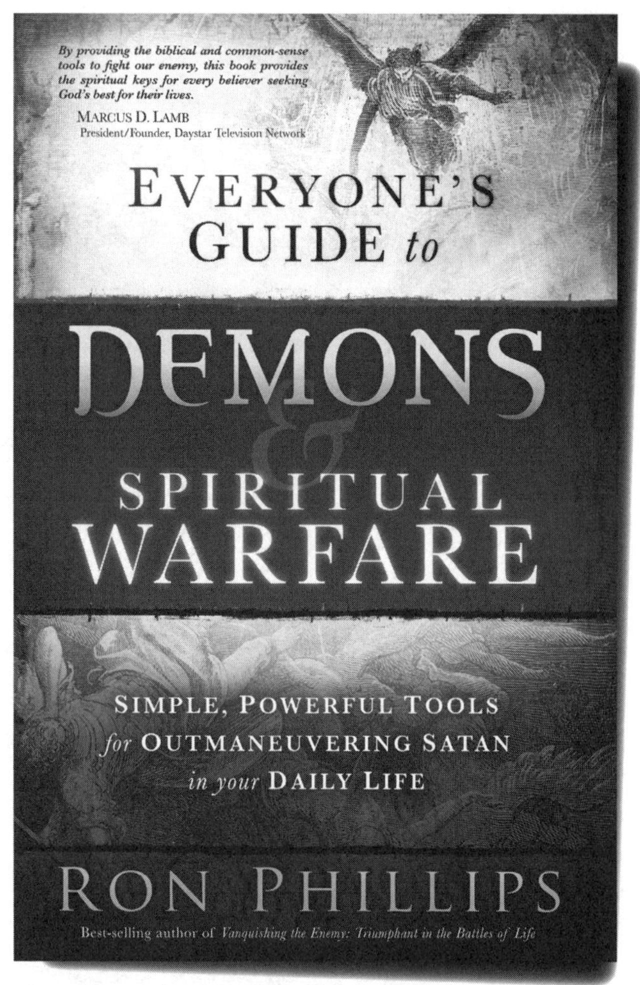
By providing the biblical and common-sense tools to fight our enemy, this book provides the spiritual keys for every believer seeking God's best for their lives.
Marcus D. Lamb
President/Founder, Daystar Television Network
EVERYONE'S GUIDE to
DEMONS
&
SPIRITUAL WARFARE
SIMPLE, POWERFUL TOOLS for OUTMANEUVERING SATAN in your DAILY LIFE
RON PHILLIPS
Best-selling author of Vanquishing the Enemy: Triumphant in the Battles of Life

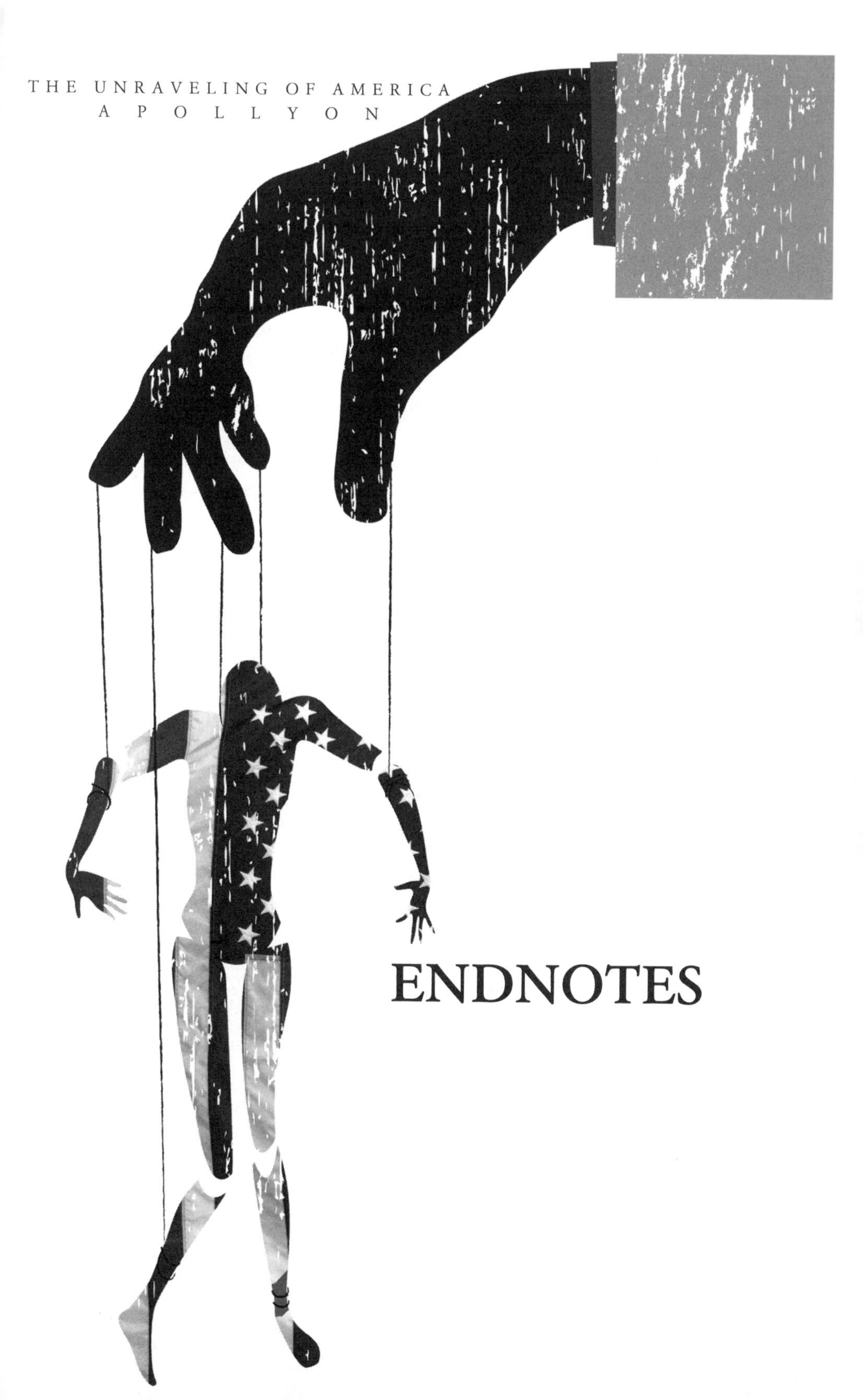
THE UNRAVELING OF AMERICA
APOLLYON
ENDNOTES

CHAPTER 1
AMERICA INVADED

1. http://www.brainyquote.com/quotes/quotes/e/edmundburk377528.html
2. https://en.wikipedia.org/wiki/Invasion
3. California Military History - California and the Second World warhttp://www.military-museum.org/HistoryWWII.html
4. https://www.jewishvirtuallibrary.org/jsource/Holocaust/goebbelslie.html
5. http://www.goodreads.com/quotes/20542-a-lie-gets-halfway-around-the-world-before-the-truth
6. http://www.wsj.com/articles/notable-quotable-edward-gibbon-on-romes-downfall-1452039902
7. http://www.gallup.com/poll/183413/americans-continue-shift-left-key-moral-issues.aspx?utm_source=liberal&utm_medium=search&utm_campaign=tiles

CHAPTER 2
WHO'S PULLING THE STRINGS?
(Unmasking the Spirit of Apollyon)

1. http://superbeefy.com/where-did-the-phrase-pulling-strings-come-from-and-what-does-the-expression-mean/
2. http://www.spiritualsatanist.com/articles/summon/apollyon.html
3. http://www.theguardian.com/world/2007/feb/01/religion.uk
4. http://www.southerncrossreview.org/24/shapero.htm
5. http://www.cnn.com/2014/02/13/world/meast/mideast-gaza-greek-statue-apollo/
6. http://www.newswithviews.com/Horn/thomas117.htm
7. http://angelsanddemons.web.cern.ch/about
8. http://www.prophecyupdate.com/cern-the-large-hadron-collider-and-bible-prophecy.html
9. Ibid.
10. http://washingtonspirits.blogspot.com/2012/10/tha-classical-architectureand-pagan.html (for a more detailed report with numerous pictures/photographs go to this web sight.)
11. http://www.cbsnews.com/news/skull-and-bones/

CHAPTER 3
TESTING THE SPIRITS
(The Spirit of Truth vs. the Spirit of Error)

1. Merriam-Webster definition of the word "gullible" @http://www.merriam-webster.com/dictionary/gullible

2. Pastor Paul Chappell writing about the history of the phrase "Acid Test." http://ministry127.com/resources/illustration/the-acid-test
3. From a sermon given by Frederick Lewis Donaldson in Westminster Abbey, London, on March 20, 1925." http://www.goodreads.com/quotes/tag/character
4. Excerpt from an article by Lynette Schaefer titled: False Prophets, Teachers and Leaders In the Laodicean Age @ http://www.raptureready.com/featured/schaefer/false.html

5. Charles Haddon Spurgeon, Lectures to My Students @ http://www.goodreads.com/quotes/tag/false-prophets
6. T. Moss. Secret's of the False Prophet's Fame, Fortune, and Success. Red Cradle Pub, LLC. PO Box 3023, Raleigh, NC 27602. Page 9.
7. Warren W. Wiersbe, The Integrity Crisis, Thomas Nelson Publishers, Nashville,TN.1988, pp. 75-76.
8. Herbert Agar quotes@http://www.quotationspage.com/quotes/Herbert_Agar/

CHAPTER 4
WHEN THE STATE BECOMES THE CHURCH
(A Wall That Never Existed)

1. https://www.law.cornell.edu/constitution/first_amendment
2. Reports of Committees of the House of Representatives Made During the First Session of the Thirty-Third Congress (Washington: A. O. P. Nicholson, 1854), pp. 6-9.http://www.wallbuilders.com/libissuesarticles.asp?id=8755#FN25
3. http://www.theblaze.com/stories/2016/01/02/heres-what-supreme-court-justice-scalia-just-said-about-religious-neutrality-the-constitution-and-why-god-has-been-good-to-america/
4. From a Fast Day Proclamation issued by Governor Samuel Adams, Massachusetts, March 20, 1797, in our possession; see also Samuel Adams, The Writings of Samuel Adams, Harry Alonzo Cushing, editor (New York: G. P. Putnam's Sons, 1908), Vol. IV, p. 407, from his proclamation of March 20, 1797. http://www.wallbuilders.com/libissuesarticles.asp?id=8755#FN25
5. Benjamin Rush, Essays, Literary, Moral & Philosophical (Philadelphia: Thomas & Samuel F. Bradford, 1798), pp. 94, 100, "A Defence of the Use of the Bible as a School Book." http://www.wallbuilders.com/libissuesarticles.asp?id=8755#FN25
6. David Barton, Separation of Church and State (What the Founders Meant). WallBuilders. P.O. Box 397 Aledo,TX 76008.2007; pg 4.
7. Read more: http://www.whatchristianswanttoknow.com/christian-presidential-quotes-22-awesome-sayings/#ixzz3ywv6s5qC
8. Ibid
9. Ibid
10.Ibid
11. David Barton, Separation of Church and State (What the Founders Meant). WallBuilders. P.O. Box 397 Aledo,TX 76008. 2007 pg 7.

12. Excerpts from George Washington's letter to the nation commonly referred to as his farewell address 1796 @http://avalon.law.yale.edu/18th_century/washing.asp
13. Excerpt of the letter from Danbury Baptist Association to newly elected President Thomas Jefferson, Oct. 7. 1801. http://www.stephenjaygould.org/ctrl/dba_jefferson.html
14. Jefferson's Letter to the Danbury Baptists @http://www.loc.gov/loc/lcib/9806/dan-pre.html
15. http://billofrightsinstitute.org/educate/educator-resources/lessons-plans/landmark-supreme-court-cases-elessons/reynolds-v-united-states-1878/
16. http://religiopoliticaltalk.blogspot.com/2007/03/separation-of-church-and-state_2805.html
17 Excerpt from the majority ruling in Stone v. Graham @thttp://www.firstamendmentschools.org/freedoms/case.aspx?id=1422
18. Excerpt from the letter written by the ACLU to the attorney of Glenview elementary school@http://www.foxnews.com/opinion/2016/01/06/school-stops-saying-god-bless-america-after-aclu-threat.html
19. Robert Spencer's analysis of President Obama's speech given at a fundamentalist mosque in Baltimore on Feb. 3,@http://www.breitbart.com/big-government/2016/02/04/2938853/

CHAPTER 5
THE AMERICAN HOLOCAUST
(The Ugly Truth About Abortion)

1. Read more: http://www.whatchristianswanttoknow.com/15-christian-quotes-against-abortion/#ixzz3zaved33W
2. Martin Niemoller quote@http://www.ushmm.org/wlc/en/article.php?ModuleId=100073
3. Of Guilt and Hope, by Martin Niemöller New York: Philosophical Library, 1947 [79 pp. 21 cm.] translation by Renee Spodheim of: Die deutsche Schuld, Not und Hoffnung,Zurich: Evangelischer Verlag, 1946.http://www.history.ucsb.edu/faculty/marcuse/projects/niem/Niem1946GuiltHope13-16.htm
4. Essence of Roe v. Wade @http://www.ontheissues.org/Background_Abortion.htm
5. Excerpt from a Speech of Mother Teresa of Calcutta to the National Prayer Breakfast, Washington, DC, February 3, 1994@http://www.priestsforlife.org/brochures/mtspeech.html
6. Abortion Statistics - United States Data & Trends@http://www.nrlc.org/uploads/factsheets/FS01AbortionintheUS.pdf
7. Abortions In America@http://www.operationrescue.org/about-abortion/abortions-in-america/
8. Former United States Surgeon General, Dr. C. Everett Koop statement about abortion protecting the life of the mother@http://www.abortionfacts.com/facts/8
9. Ibid
10. Pro-choice group cries foul over Doritos commercial

'Ultrasound'@http://www.foxnews.com/us/2016/02/08/pro-choice-group-cries-foul-over-doritos-commercial-ultrasound.html
11. Why Does Planned Parenthood Get $3.6 Billion in Tax Dollars When it Makes $700 Million From Abortions?@http://www.lifenews.com/2015/03/03/why-does-planned-parenthood-get-3-6-billion-in-tax-dollars-when-it-makes-700-million-from-abortions/
12. For more than 30 years, the Hyde Amendment has prevented federal tax dollars from being used to pay for Medicaid abortions. The Hyde Amendment is a rider which has been annually included in the appropriations bill for the Department of Health and Human Services since 1976. It prevents the DHHS from spending tax dollars on abortion. However, with the upcoming implementation of President Obama's health care reform law, new routes for abortion funding and subsidizing have been opened up.@http://www.rtl.org/RLMNews/09editions/AreMyTaxDollarsPayingForAbortion.htm
13. Obama answers a question on CNN's edition of BALLOT BOWL 2008@ http://transcripts.cnn.com/TRANSCRIPTS/0803/29/bb.01.html
14. Texas grand jury clears Planned Parenthood, indicts its accusers@http://www.cnn.com/2016/01/25/politics/planned-parenthood-activists-indicted/
(Note: You can go to http://www.centerformedicalprogress.org/author/david/and view all the videos. While there may be differences of opinion on how the videos were obtained, I personally believe they show beyond a doubt the corruption that exist at Planned Parenthood. View the videos and make up your own mind.)
15. The Spirit of Cain: Abortion and Murder by Robin Schumacher@http://www.blogos.org/compellingtruth/abortion-murder.html
16. Ibid
17. Ibid

CHAPTER 6
THE BIG MYTH
(Islam is a Religion of Peace)

1. The Word Islam Means Peace@Read more at http://www.brainyquote.com/quotes/quotes/m/muhammadal643397.html#hUZYAvrdhhsKABO7.99
2. Hillary Clinton defends Islam, says it's a religion of peace and that Muslims have nothing to do with terrorism@http://www.christiantoday.com/article
3. Definition of Myth@http://www.merriam-webster.com/dictionary/myth
4. John F. Kennedy quotes@http://refspace.com/quotes/John_F_Kennedy/Q1898
5. For more detailed information about how to engage Muslims with the gospel of Jesus Christ I urge you to purchase my book, "The Hiram Code." It may be purchased through our website, and most Christian bookstores.
6. The Thomas Jefferson Papers, 1606 to 1827- General Correspondence. 1651-1827, pp. 430-432.@https://www.loc.gov/collections/thomas-jefferson-papers/about-this-collection/

7. "Islam is Peace" Says President. Remarks by the President at Islamic Center of Washington, D.C.@http://georgewbush-whitehouse.archives.gov/news/releases/2001/09/20010917-11.html
8. Obama: Islam is a religion of 'peace, charity and justice' selected remarks quoted from http://www.christiantoday.com/article/obama.islam.is.a.religion.of.peace.charity.and.justice/79033.htm
9. People know the consequences: Opposing view@http://www.usatoday.com/story/opinion/2015/01/07/islam-allah-muslims-shariah-anjem-choudary-editorials-debates
10. These examples were taken from a variety of sources. You can find more information@http://www.wnd.com/2015/07/shooters-motive-stumps-obama-fbi-media/
11. Obama said in 2008 that he planned to "Fundamentally Transform America." He has remained true to that promise@http://www.nowtheendbegins.com/barack-obama-plans-destroy-united-states-america/
12. Rosen: Obama's claim that "Islam is a religion of peace" is a fantasy@http://www.denverpost.com/opinion/ci_27798465/religion-peace-fantasy
13. 'Islam Is Not a Peaceful Religion': Evangelist Franklin Graham's Warning About What Might Happen If 'We Continue to Allow Muslim Immigration'@http://www.theblaze.com/stories/2015/
14. Excerpts from Text: Obama's Speech in Cairo@http://www.nytimes.com/2009/06/04/us/politics/04obama.text.html
15. Sura 5:32-33@ http://quran.com/5/32-33
16. Selected quotes by Ibn Kathir@ http://www.qtafsir.com/index.php
17. Sura 9:29@http://quran.com/9/29
18. Ibid
19. Sahih Muslim Book 1 Hadith 30@https://muflihun.com/muslim/1/30
20. Excerpted from: "Islam is not a religion of peace": Ayaan Hirsi Ali@http://www.salon.com/2015/04/04/islam_is_not_a_religion_of_peace_ayaan_hirsi_ali/
21. Nancy Pelosi Quotes Mohammad and Pushes Islam at the National Prayer Breakfast@http://eaglerising.com/29907/nancy-pelosi-quotes-mohammad-and-pushes-islam-at-the-national-prayer-breakfast/
22. These are just a few examples. They are taken from Jesus and Muhammad, Islam and Christianity: A Side-by-Side Comparison. For more insight and details go to:http://www.thereligionofpeace.com/pages/articles/jesus-muhammad.aspx
23. Muslim Belief Is 'Closer to the Teaching of Christ' Than Some Churches, Says Christian Pastor@http://www.breitbart.com/national-security/2016/02/16/muslim-belief-is-closer-to-the-teaching-of-christ-than-some-churches-says-christian-pastor/
24 Visions of Jesus Stir Muslim Hearts@http://www1.cbn.com/onlinediscipleship/visions-of-jesus-stir-muslim-hearts

CHAPTER 7
THE GRAND ILLUSION
(The "Hoax" of Borrowing Your Way to Wealth)

1. Winston S. Churchill quotes@http://www.goodreads.com/author/show/14033.Winston_S_Churchill
2. The Madoff Pyramid (2008)@http://www.cbsnews.com/media/top-14-financial-frauds-of-all-time/14/
3. Joe Biden: 'We Have to Go Spend Money to Keep From Going Bankrupt' spoken at a town hall in Alexandria, VA@http://caps.fool.com/Blogs/joe-biden-we-have-to-go/229577
4. National Debt Tops $18 Trillion: Guess How Much You Owe? by Mike Patton@http://www.forbes.com/sites/mikepatton/2015/04/24/national-debt-tops-18-trillion-guess-how-much-you-owe/
5. These numbers are from 2014. They are constantly changing but this gives an idea of the amount of our debt@http://www.theblaze.com/stories/2013/10/12/chart-who-does-the-u-s-govt-owe-17-trillion-to/
6. Margaret Thatcher quotes on Socialism@http://www.snopes.com/politics/quotes/thatcher.asp
7. Thomas Jefferson Warned Us About Socialism@http://lubbockonline.com/interact/blog-post/donald-r-may/2014-05-19/thomas-jefferson-warned-us-about-socialism#.VtHI8sd0tT5
8. Ibid
9. Martin Bormann, Reich Leader, 1942, 'National Socialist and Christian Concepts are Incompatible', From Kirchliches Jahrbuch fur die evangelische Kirche in Deutschland, 1933-1944, pp. 470-472, quoted pp. 245-247, George L. Mosse, Nazi Culture: A Documentary History.@http://christsassembly.com/literature/
10. What Does Haiti Have to Show for $13 Billion in Earthquake Aid? by TRACY CONNOR, HANNAH RAPPLEYE and ERIKA ANGULO@http://www.nbcnews.com/news/investigations/what-does-haiti-have-show-13-billion-earthquake-aid
11. Food Stamp Beneficiaries Exceed 46,000,000 for 38 Straight Months@http://www.cnsnews.com/news/article/ali-meyer/food-stamp-beneficiaries-exceed-46000000-38-straight-months
12. Famous Quotes About Food Stamps@http://topfamousquotes.com/quotes-about-food-stamps/
13. Borrowing Your Way Out of Debt and Other Normal Abnormalities by Bill Bonner@http://dailyreckoning.com/borrowing-your-way-out-of-debt-and-other-normal-abnormalities/
14. Top 100 Inspirational Quotes@http://www.forbes.com/sites/kevinkruse/2013/05/28/inspirational-quotes/#4e6da5136697

CHAPTER 8
SHOWDOWN
(Exposing the Homosexual Agenda)

1. Then Minnesota State Senator and former US Congresswoman Michele Bachmann, speaking at EdWatch National Education Conference, November 6, 2004@ http://www.thenewcivilrightsmovement.com/michele-bachmanns-top-ten-anti-gay-quotes/politics/2011/06/02/21233
2. Much of the source material for the outline of the 6 Point strategic plan of Kirk and Medsen is excerpted from the article written by Charles Melear: Gay Agenda Blueprint A Plan The to Transform America Posted on Sep 15, 2015 For more details go to http://www.ucg.org/the-good-news/the-gay-agenda-blueprint-a-plan-to-transform-america)
3 - 12 Ibid
13. PUBLIC SCHOOLS BEGINNING TO TEACH HOMOSEXUALITY: IT IS HIGH TIME FOR CHRISTIAN PARENTS TO PULL THEIR PRECIOUS CHILDREN OUT!@http://www.cuttingedge.org/news/
14. Obama appoints Homosexual Propagandist to Education By Steve Baldwin, Western-Journalism.com Exclusive@http://www.westernjournalism.com/exclusive-investigative-reports/obama-appoints-homosexual-propogandist-to-education/
15. Media-Censored: Top 15 Quotes from Justices AGAINST Gay Marriage@http://www.newsbusters.org/blogs/katie-yoder/2015/06/29/media-censored-top-15-quotes-justices-against-gay-marriage
16. Gender Identity Curriculum Angers Parents in Virginia byCharlene Aaron@http://www1.cbn.com/cbnnews/us/2015/June/Gender-Identity-Curriculum-Angers-Parents-in-Fairfax
17. Hollywood: Driving the Homosexual Agenda for 40 Years By Paul Wilson | May 10, 2012@http://newsbusters.org/blogs/paul-wilson/2012/05/10/hollywood-driving-homosexual-agenda-40-years
18. 3 Other Christian Denominations That Allow Gay Marriage by Nolan Feeney March 18, 2015@http://time.com/3749253/churches-g ay-marriage/
19. Ibid
20. Meet The Evangelicals Who Cheered The SCOTUS Gay Marriage Ruling@http://www.huffingtonpost.com/2015/06/29/evangelical-christians-support-marriage-equality
21. Ibid

CHAPTER 9
IS POLITICAL CORRECTNESS DESTROYING AMERICA?

1. Remarks on the 20th Anniversary of the Voice of America; Department of Health, Education, and Welfare, February 26, 1962]@Read more: http://www.whatchristianswanttoknow.com/bible-verses-about-truth-20-great-scripture-quotes/#ixzz422HfIn4c
2. The Inconvenient Facts the Media Ignore About Climate Change by Rep. Lamar Smith@http://dailysignal.com
3. Can the media be trusted? By Talha Wani Published: February 23, 2015@http://tribune.com.pk/story/842506/can-the-media-be-trusted/
4. The Terrible Truth About Walter Cronkite by Cliff Kincaid — July 20, 2009@http://www.aim.org/aim-column/the-terrible-truth-about-walter-cronkite/
5. Definition of Political Correctness@http://www.urbandictionary.com/define.php?term=politically+correct
6. What is Political Correctness@http://www.conservapedia.com/Politically_correct
7. Ibid
8. Read more of Martin Daubney's article: Was 2014 the year political correctness went stark raving mad?@http://www.telegraph.co.uk/men/thinking-man/11294974/Was-2014-the-year-political-correctness-went-stark-raving-mad.html
9. What is Political Correctness@http://www.conservapedia.com/Politically_correct
10. Roger Kimball quotes@http://www.goodreads.com/quotes/tag/political-correctness
11. Excerpted from "Sick of hearing about pampered students with coddled minds? This university president is" @https://www.washingtonpost.com/news/answer-sheet/
12. This is Not a Day Care. It's a University! by Dr. Everett Piper, President Oklahoma Wesleyan University@http://www.okwu.edu/blog/2015/11/this-is-not-a-day-care-its-a-university/
13. For comprehensive details about the "list of demands" and the complete response from Western Washington U. President go to: https://www.insidehighered.com/news/2016/03/10/western-washington-university-students-push-sweeping-demands
14. Excerpted from an article: 19 SHOCKING EXAMPLES OF HOW POLITICAL CORRECTNESS IS DESTROYING AMERICA@http://www.infowars.com/19-shocking-examples-of-how-political-correctness-is-destroying-america/
15. Ibid
16. Excerpted from an article: What a Texas City Is Demanding These Pastors Do With Their Sermons About Homosexuality@http://www.theblaze.com/stories/2014
17. Almost 1,600 Pastors Defy IRS, Preach Politics From Pulpit by Steven Ertelt - October 8,2012@http://www.lifenews.com/2012/10/08/almost-1600-pastors-defy-irs-preach-politics-from-pulpit/

CHAPTER 10
CONSPIRACY OF SILENCE
(Things the Mainstream Media Doesn't Want You to Know)

1. Truth Quotes:
@http://www.brainyquote.com/quotes/quotes/m/marcusaure143088.html?src=t_truth
2. Hillary Clinton Pushes Abortion in First Speech as Candidate: Too Many Women "Denied" Abortions: Steven Ertelt, April 24,2015@http://www.lifenews.com/2015/04/24/hillary-clinton-pushes-abortion-in-first-speech-as-candidate-too-many-women-denied-abortion/
3. Excerpted from "Media Bias"@https://www.studentnewsdaily.com/types-of-media-bias/
4. The above information is excerpted and adapted from How to Identify Liberal Media Bias by Brent H. Baker, Vice President for Research and Publications at Media Research Center.@https://www.studentnewsdaily.com/types-of-media-bias/
5. The Top Ten Reasons were excerpted from "The Top 10 Reasons George Soros Is Dangerous:" to read more details go to http://humanevents.com/2011/04/02/top-10-reasons-george-soros-is-dangerous/
6. Read more at:
http://www.brainyquote.com/quotes/quotes/j/johncolema409264.html?src=t_global_warming
7. Read more at:
http://www.brainyquote.com/quotes/quotes/d/diannefein411942.html?src=t_global_warming
8. Making terrorism link, Obama says climate instability can lead to 'dangerous' ideology@https://www.washingtonpost.com/news/energy-environment/wp/2015/12/04/making-terrorism-link-obama-says-climate-instability-can-lead-to-dangerous-ideology/
9. Ibid
10. Attorney General Lynch Looks Into Prosecuting 'Climate Change Deniers' By Hans von Spakovsky | March 11, 2016@http://www.cnsnews.com/commentary/hans-von-spakovsky/attorney-general-lynch-looks-prosecuting-climate-change-deniers
11. Ibid
12. Black Lives Matter issues MAJOR THREAT to white people over presidential election Written by The Analytical Economist on March 18, 2016@http://www.allenbwest.com/2016/03/black-lives-matter-issues-major-threat-to-white-people-over-presidential-election/
13. 5 Truths Covered Up or Ignored by Phony Black Lives Matter Movement@http://www.breitbart.com/big-government/2015/08/12/5-truths-covered-up-or-ignored-by-phony-black-lives-matter-movement/
14. Ibid
15. Ibid
16. Ibid
17. Ibid
18. UNREAL: Look what Black Lives Matter is calling RACIST now Written by The Analytical Economist on February 25, 2016@http://www.allenbwest.com/2016/02/ridicu-

lous-blacklives-matter-co-founder-now-says-this-is-racist/
19. Why don't we hear about persecuted Christians? By Natasha Moore Updated 1 Aug 2014 @http://www.abc.net.au/news/2014-08-01/moore-why-don't-we-hear-about-persecuted-christians/5641390
20. Ibid
21.The Rev. Franklin Graham of Samaritans Purse visited the Middle East and told Megyn Kelly on Fox News about the plight of Christians@http://www.newsmax.com/FastFeatures/middle-east-christians/2015/05/12/id/644027/
22. Under Mounting Pressure, Kerry Declares Islamic State Has Committed Genocide@http://www.breitbart.com/national-security/2016/03/17/under-mounting-pressure-kerry-finally-declares-islamic-state-genocide-against-christians-minorities/
23.Beheadings, imprisonment made 2015 worst year for Christian persecution, report finds By Perry Chiaramonte Published March 08, 2016@http://www.foxnews.com/world/2016/03/08/beheadings-imprisonment-made-2015-worst-year-for-christian-persecution-report-finds.html
24.Breaking News at Newsmax.com http://www.newsmax.com/FastFeatures/middle-east-christians/2015/05/12/id/644027/#ixzz43Ynax6in

CHAPTER 11
BEHIND THE VEIL
(Exposing the Deception of Sharia Law)

1. Muammar Kaddafi (1997, after meeting with Louis Farrakhan)@http://topfamousquotes.com/quotes-about-sharia/
2. Ibid
3. Obama: Attending Cuba Baseball Game with Castro Sends Message to Terrorists@http://www.breitbart.com/big-government/2016/03/22/obama-attending-cuba-baseball-game-with-castro-a-sign-of-resilience/
4. Refugee Watch Warns: 'Brussels Coming To A Town Near You'@http://www.breitbart.com/big-government/2016/03/22/refugee-watch-warns-brussels-coming-to-a-town-near-you/
5. William Muir quotes@ http://www.azquotes.com/author/30024-William_Muir
6. Excerpted and adapted from Sharia law for non-Muslims by Bill Warner at the center for the study of political Islam. Copyright 2010. Published by www.cspipublishing.com
7. Where Do Muslims Really Stand on Shariah Law? Global Study Provides Fascinating Revelations@http://www.theblaze.com/stories/2013/05/01/study-where-do-muslims-really-stand-on-shariah-law/
8. Spread of Islam-Islam Spreading in Five Phases@http://www.billionbibles.org/sharia/islam-expansion.html (An excellent resource for the serious minded who want to find out what is really going on behind the veil of deception)
9. Exerted and adapted from an article entitled "Sharia Law in America-Sharia Law Advancing in America"@http://www.billionbibles.org/sharia/america-sharia-law.html

10.Did You Know There Are Muslim 'No-Go' Zones In The USA@http://truthuncensored.net/there-are-muslim-no-go-zones-in-the-usa/
11. Ibid
12. Islamization of America - Accelerating Islamization of America@http://www.billionbibles.org/sharia/islamization-of-america.html
13. Ibid
14. Exerted an adapted from Muslim Brotherhood Project, Exposing The Muslim Brotherhood Manifesto@http://www.billionbibles.org/sharia/muslim-brotherhood-project.html
15. Neville Chamberlain quotes@: http://www.brainyquote.com/quotes/quotes/n/nevillecha195587.html
16. Ibid

CHAPTER 12
HOPE IN THE MIDST OF ANCIENT HATE
(A Message of Hope to a Fearful World)

1. Martin Luther King Jr. A Testament of Hope: The Essential Writings and Speeches@http://www.goodreads.com/quotes/tag/hate
2. Adapted and excerpted from an article titled: Anti-Semitism: The only hate allowed in campus 'safe spaces' By Lawrence Summers April 2, 2016@http://nypost.com/2016/04/02/anti-semitism-the-only-hate-allowed-in-campus-safe-spaces/
3. Ibid
4. Sir Winston Churchill; (Source: The River War, first edition, Vol II, pages 248-250 London).